ENOUGH

of me

In her book, *Enough of Me*, Priscilla Peters connects with what almost every woman, including me, has felt at some point in our lives. We are often filled up on what the world thinks is important, tired from the incessant rat race to grab and get all we can, pulled at every turn to be better and do better yet, we still feel empty inside. Priscilla gives us the key to a fulfilled life by reminding us that true joy and fulfillment comes when we live on God's mission and not our own. And let me tell you, she doesn't have a boring bone in her body! Priscilla uses her spunk, wit, and realness to connect to each woman in our everyday lives. One minute you will laugh (a lot) and the next you will cry as a point hits home. Priscilla's honesty with her own journey makes it easy to relate to the struggles we all face as women. She shares her desire to find freedom from the everyday expected life to the blessing of being on God's mission. When you have had enough of trying it on your own, grab this book and get on God's mission! You will love the freedom it brings!

—STACEY HARNESS
Real Women Leader

an 8-week Bible study

ENOUGH
of me

winning the tug-of-war
between our *flesh* and our *mission*

priscilla peters

AMBASSADOR INTERNATIONAL
GREENVILLE, SOUTH CAROLINA & BELFAST, NORTHERN IRELAND

www.ambassador-international.com

Enough of Me

Winning the Tug of War Between Our Flesh and Our Mission

ISBN: 978-1-62020-819-9
eISBN: 978-1-62020-825-0

Cover Design & Typesetting by Hannah Nichols
Ebook Conversion by Anna Riebe Raats

AMBASSADOR INTERNATIONAL
Emerald House
411 University Ridge, Suite B14
Greenville, SC 29601, USA
www.ambassador-international.com

AMBASSADOR BOOKS
The Mount
2 Woodstock Link
Belfast, BT6 8DD, Northern Ireland, UK
www.ambassadormedia.co.uk

The colophon is a trademark of Ambassador

In loving memory of my beloved Aunt Jan

Contents

INTRODUCTION

I LOVE MY FANCY-PANTS WORLD. I really do. It's cozy, and fun, and exactly what I hoped it would be—full of Netflix binges, Target runs, a swanky-swank career, and a family calendar that stacks up to any Mom-of-the-Year candidate I know.

I'm living the dream, and I've got the Instagram feed to prove it.

Who am I kidding?

I'm literally holding it together with one more cup of coffee, yesterday's dry shampoo, and a prayer.

I'm exhausted—tired of playing the comparison game and worn-out of pretending.

I'm realizing this fancy-pants world I've built is meaningless.

So I finally said enough.

Enough of me.

This was after over a decade of harassment from the Holy Spirit mind you, but I'm fighting daily to surrender the pursuit of emptiness and replace it with a thirst for all that is Jesus and the mission that is mine in His name.

I'm bidding farewell to chasing emptiness and exchanging it for more of Jesus.

And, you can too.

Maybe you're like me—exhausted, worn-out, empty, and overwhelmed. Who could get busy for Jesus in this state?

Girl, I hear ya! But I also know we were made for more.

Together, I believe we can identify what is holding us back and finally say enough to all of it. Maybe for you it's a load of excuses and baggage you're carrying around in that handbag you had to have. Or, maybe you're like me and for years you've been navigating life in limbo—satisfied with just enough Jesus to make you content. We've got the Jesus t-shirt and the praying-hands emoji locked and loaded—what else does a girl really need?

We all have barriers in our lives that stand between where we are today and where God wants to use us to finish His work.

> But my life is worth nothing to me unless I use it for finishing the work assigned me by the Lord Jesus—the work of telling others the Good News about the wonderful grace of God. – Acts 20:24 (NLT)

I'm inviting you on a quest.

Let's take a deep breath and do some inventory.

Let's dig in and see what God's Word has to say about the tug-of-war between our flesh and our mission.

Let's figure out practical ways to quit chasing emptiness and take bold steps of obedience.

Let's discover how we can glorify God and steer people to Jesus—in our workplace, at our dinner tables, in our mom-groups, at the park, and with the people we encounter every day.

Prepare yourself. I'm pretty sure we will be challenged by the Holy Spirit in the best possible way, and it will most likely require a move outside of our comfort zones. I feel confident there will be toes stepped on and maybe a few tearful face-plants into those sheets of ours that might not have been washed this week.

But I know this quest can be life changing, shifting our focus from ourselves to the one that means and is everything.

I can promise you lots of laughs—there is no shame in my game.

I assure you honesty in sharing my own journey of bidding farewell to chasing emptiness.

And, my prayer is that it all be anchored in Jesus.

I can't wait to see what happens when we say enough of me. More of Jesus.

Priscilla

Week 1:

Enough *people-pleasing*. More PLEASING HIM.

For they loved the approval of men rather than the approval of God.

– John 12:43 (NASB)

I JUST LOVE WHEN THE heat of summer turns into the crispness of fall. Two years ago, it was that time of year when September slips into October, college football is on the television, and fall fashion has its first reveal of the season. I was attending a women's conference at one of the largest churches in my area. A group of my make-me-laugh-until-I-hurt friends had set aside the weekend to hang out, get closer to Jesus, and stay up super-late in the room we got with our hotel points.

No kids. No husbands. Lots of laughs and plenty of caffeine and calories.

I walked in the conference that first Friday night and the aroma of high-dollar perfume and the sea of handbags I'd dreamed of purchasing over the past few months hit me with a gust of jealousy and envy I could control—but I'm not gonna lie, it did shake me a bit. Then I looked down, and a tornado blew me over.

Flip flops and sandals had been retired from these parts for the season. They had been replaced with booties—peep toe, ankle high, wedge, flat, high heel—you name it, and there's a bootie for you. I was in love. But I didn't get the memo. I was sporting my best suede wedges from Target that I felt super-confident about before entering into this world of fashionistas, but clearly I didn't measure up.

I was obsessed.

I literally logged on to Amazon during the opening "fun" time when we were supposed to be getting to know each other and making connections that would last an eternity. Sorry gals, I'm checking my bank balance and wondering if I can get overnight shipping on these peep-toe booties I found. More importantly, I was wondering what kind of bartering I would have to do to get my husband to bring them to me so I can at least measure up for the final day of the conference and gain back some dignity.

I know. It's lame. And shallow. And a little disturbing. I was entangled in a shoe catastrophe.

Here I was, entering in to this place where I should be preparing to meet the King of Kings, and I'm caught up in a footwear frenzy. I'm not sure there was any escaping.

Halfway through the worship set God had enough.

I lost service on my phone after ignoring a nudge or two from my girlfriends (can I please get some support from my own squad?!), so I put down my phone. However, I did not put down the people-pleasing, comparison game-playing emotions that were running rampant in my head. I was on a mind train to Crazytown right in the middle of thousands of Jesus girls who were ready for all God had for them that weekend.

I, on the other hand, was praying UPS delivered to the Fairfield Inn on Saturdays.

Does the people-pleasing, comparison game ever trip you up? Maybe you're like me, and the desire to be liked, adored, and praised by others overwhelms you to the core.

We can't even begin to carry out the mission God called us to with a people-pleasing agenda on full throttle.

I want to be like her—that skinny, sweet, never loses her temper, flawless husband and perfect kids, never a bad hair day, picture of perfection. If I can't be her, I'll just pretend to be.

With the help of the enemy, I've painted this picture of perfection I strive to achieve; because, if I'm more like her (and less like me), then everyone will like me, look up to me, admire me, and envy *me*. And it will be awesome.

I think.

I've never been there, so I wouldn't know, but surely it would be epic.

Living out loud as who we really are is a bold step, sister. But we can't even begin to carry out the mission God called us to with a people-pleasing agenda on full throttle.

So, what's a bootie-obsessed girl to do? (I see the irony in this statement, but I'm just going to carry on and assume we all understand we're talking shoes here and not backsides— that would be for another day.)

We've been riding this mind train of obsession for way too long.

It's time to say enough people-pleasing.

Enough pretending.

Enough of me.

The Comparison Game

For am I now seeking the favor of men, or of God? Or am I striving to please men? If I were still trying to please men, I would not be a bond-servant of Christ.

– Galatians 1:10 (NASB)

TAKE IT FROM ME, PEOPLE-PLEASING is exhausting. And exhaustion holds us back from getting busy for Jesus.

So, how do we really say enough pretending when our comparison game is on-point? We make the decision to choose God over everything and everyone else in our everyday moments. Otherwise, we're accidentally putting our hope in anything and anyone else.

Sisters Mary and Martha epitomized this tug-of-war within our hearts and minds in Luke 10, arguably one of the most popular Scripture passages for women of our time—a passage that embodies the truth in this struggle. I don't think we can read it enough.

> As Jesus and the disciples continued on their way to Jerusalem, they came to a certain village where a woman named Martha welcomed him into her home. Her sister, Mary, sat at the Lord's feet, listening to what he taught. But Martha was distracted by the big dinner she was preparing. She came to Jesus and said, "Lord, doesn't it seem unfair to you that my sister just sits here while I do all the work? Tell her to come and help me."

> But the Lord said to her, "My dear Martha, you are worried and upset over all these details! There is only one thing worth being concerned about. Mary has discovered it, and it will not be taken away from her." – Luke 10:38-42 (NLT)

We are so "worried and upset" about the meaningless. For Martha it was a Pinterest-worthy dinner table and being the hostess with the *mostest*. For me, on that early fall evening smack dab in the middle of where God wanted to meet me, I was distracted with visions of peep-toe, ankle-high shoe perfection that would define me better in the ranks of all those women. #ICantHang

What about you? What consumes you?

What has you "worried and upset," distracted from sitting at the feet of Jesus and listening to what He has to say?

Prayerfully consider these two questions and jot down your thoughts here.

_____

_____

_____

_____

_____

_____

Somewhere along the way, the enemy has joined us in creating this people-pleasing value system, where significance lives in measuring up and impressing so-and-so. Ultimately, striving to please our Creator should be the value we're chasing.

On the scale below put an "x" where you think you land in this conundrum of pleasing people or pleasing God. Do you tend to defer to pleasing others or are you focused on pleasing God and bringing Him glory?

Pleasing People_____Pleasing God

Fill in the blanks:

Do not_____ to the pattern of this world, but be _____ by the renewing of your mind. Then you will be able

to test and approve what God's will is—his good, _____
and perfect will. – Romans 12:2 (NIV)

Who specifically (besides God) do you put value in pleasing the most?
(Circle the 2 most common.)

Friends   Family   Church buddies

Coworkers   Strangers (people you want to be like)

Acquaintances (you wish were besties)

> Those who belong to Christ Jesus have nailed the passions and desires
> of their sinful nature to his cross and crucified them there. Since we
> are living by the Spirit, let us follow the Spirit's leading in every part
> of our lives. Let us not become conceited, or provoke one another, or
> be jealous of one another. – Galatians 5:24-26 (NLT)

Consider the "passions and desires" you struggle with that need to be nailed
to the cross. Check the response(s) that best fit you.

O I'm obsessed with what others are thinking and saying about me.

O I'm consumed with the way I look (what I wear, my hair color, jewelry,
   body image, etc.)

O I'm constantly comparing myself to others and often feeling like I'll
   never measure up.

O I'm really good at pretending I have it all together on the outside, but
   on the inside I feel like I'm hanging by a thread.

What consumes us defines us.

When we're caught up in these passions, worries, and desires, we're creating
barriers that restrict us from focusing on Jesus and navigating others to Him.

The battle to stay caught up in the comparison game is real. And so is
the enemy.

> Stay alert! Watch out for your great enemy, the devil. He
> prowls around like a roaring lion, looking for someone to
> devour. – 1 Peter 5:8 (NLT)

The enemy is real. He and his legion are hell-bent on planting thoughts in our heads that get us all out of focus. The evil one loves to seep into the cracks of our humanity and sprinkle his lies into our internal dialogue. Some days it gets out of hand—fast!

The super bowl of the comparison game is played out on our social media newsfeeds every day. If we're not careful, the highlight reels of our friends and followers hijack our thoughts and consume us in every possible way.

As I'm writing this, it's the first official week of summer, and the vacation posts in my Facebook feed have me in a funk. I have friends in Costa Rica, Turks and Caicos, the Gulf Coast, and various other fabulous vacay destinations. Meanwhile, I'm unloading the car from our staycation an hour south of our home. Tiny umbrella drinks and poolside service were not on the menu. #ArkansasPartyof7

I'm caught up in it all—focusing on how I can make a humble lake house look like an all-inclusive resort in the Caribbean through Instagram filters and selfies with just the right angle. I'm chasing likes, comments, and shares, instead of chasing a God that's sitting back waiting for the whistle to blow on this comparison game.

Here's what I've learned about the comparison game:

I will never win.

It's no fun. Ever.

Even on the off-chance that I do win a round, it feels icky and does not fulfill me.

It's exhausting, demoralizing, and toxic to my soul.

When I surrender my spot as the MVP of the comparison game, I can breathe. I can finally fulfill my duties on the roster I was meant to play for, in a game focused on eternities.

When I surrender my spot as the MVP of the comparison game, I can breathe.

ENOUGH SAID: AFTER READING TODAY'S lesson, let's capture a truth and take a step in obedience.

What did you hear God specifically say to you today through His Word?

_____

_____

_____

_____

How will you respond?

_____

_____

The Best Stocking Stuffer Ever

On hearing this, Jesus said to them, "It is not the healthy who need a doctor,
but the sick. I have not come to call the righteous, but sinners."

– Mark 2:17 (NIV)

I TURNED FORTY, AND IT happened. All of a sudden, my eyes began failing me.

One day I was basking in the joy of my 20/20 vision, and the next I was questioning everything in front of me. And for about forty-eight hours (before I realized it was my eyes failing me and not my mental capacity), I experienced all kinds of humiliation. I collected a lifetime of stories to tell during "share your most embarrassing moment" exercises.

Matter of fact, I was attending a marketing conference in Dallas when it first hit me. I was alone, which is completely out-of-the-ordinary for most of my work travel, but I was hobnobbing with other advertising executives, so I still felt like I was with my people.

Truth be told, if I *had* been with my coworkers, there would have been t-shirts made commemorating the events of the next forty-eight hours. There would have been belly laughs complete with tears and no living it down. Ever.

Thank you, Jesus, I was alone on this particular trip!

Because I never meet a stranger, I scooted in to the opening session of the conference with an energetic "Is this seat taken?" at the hippest table I could find. If there's one thing I've learned over the past few years in the advertising business, it's stick with the hipsters. They're going places, and they have a bold respect for those of us who have been-there-done-that if you're open to their dreams and vision.

And they wear jeans everywhere—jeans are my fancy-pants, so I'm in.

The morning's speaker was discussing all things "content marketing" with his spiel full of buzzwords that would leave any marketer drooling. I was enamored with what he was saying, but frustrated at the lack of attention the conference staff was attributing to his actual visual presentation. One of the perks of attending an advertising and marketing conference is you are rarely presented with a PowerPoint complete with bullet points and clip art. We are professionals, and our presentations are badges of honor.

Except on this morning, the presentation was seriously out of focus.

I leisurely leaned over to the full-bearded millennial on my right, and said, "You would think the conference team would be sure the presentation is in focus. We *are* in marketing aren't we?" To which he gave me a weird look and took a sip of coffee.

Clearly, he was not a morning person.

So, after a few more minutes, I leaned over to the beautiful princess with perfect-hair on my left and said, "What is the deal with these projectors? Should we be sure someone from the conference staff knows everything is out of focus?"

"Ummmmm . . . they're in focus," she said. And I got a nod from her neighbor confirming everything on the screens was indeed in focus, and I had a new problem on my hands.

I just wasn't ready to admit it.

Welcome to forty, ladies. Happy birthday to me!

For the next two days, I was fighting an internal battle of disbelief that I could no longer make out information on a screen the size of Texas less than twenty-five feet from me, much less read a menu right in front of my face.

So when I flew home, I went straight to the eye doctor. One pair of no-line bifocals later, I was back. Well, kind of.

It took me about two weeks to adjust to my new face gear. Staircases were a problem—we'll just leave it at that. #FacePlant

My six-year-old daughter immediately wanted to wear my glasses every minute of the day. It was driving me nuts.

With Christmas right around the corner, it was time for me to pile up on stocking stuffers for my crew. I knew one thing for sure would be going in the stocking labeled "Stella" for my six-year-old pistol.

Fake glasses.

A quick trip to Claire's, and those bad-boys were stuffed in that stocking hung by the chimney with care. Christmas morning I would get my own glasses back and she could strut her stuff in her new digs.

It happened perfectly as planned. However, it went on a little longer than planned.

To be honest, it's the middle of June. Yes, six months and three pairs of seven dollar glasses later (let's be real, they weren't meant for every day wear), she's still (to this day) sporting the fake glasses.

I have answered the question "Oh, when did Stella get glasses?" more than I can count, and if I hear "It's just not normal" from my dad one more time, I'm going to lose it.

I had no idea the charade would go on this long. In her mind, I honestly don't think she's looking at it as "pretending" she needs glasses. She just likes the glasses and thinks it's fun to wear them.

I have to admit, the glasses have been fantastic for parenting leverage.

Have you ever grounded your kid from fake glasses? I've checked that box a time or two over the past few months. #MomOfTheYear

She's worn the glasses so much that in her heart the pretending is turning into her normal. What was fun and trendy for a while is now a crutch of must-have she clings to every day. We are working on it. But pray for me. I'm running out of solutions on this one. And, when your biggest fear is that Claire's is going to stop carrying the kid frames your six-year-old has to have, you are in trouble. Big time.

For my six-year-old sassy-pants it's fake glasses, but what is it for me?

It's pretending to have it *all* together.

Every single bit of it.

I'm living in marital bliss.

I'm making that money.

My kids are angels of perfection.

My house is immaculate and all that Joanna Gaines would want it to be.

I run with enthusiasm to my quiet time with God every day.

My pantry is full of non-GMO, organic flawlessness.

Oh the pretending. The lies I live.

My reality is . . .

At Camp Peters we live paycheck to paycheck.

In a good month, all the sheets in my household get washed. Once.

Sometimes I dread praying.

Someone in my tribe was throat-punched in the car on the way to church last week.

I have dry spells apart from the Word.

Little Debbie is a frequent visitor in my snack drawer.

Take a minute and jot down areas in your life where you're pretending:

_____

_____

_____

_____

_____

Pretending forces our hearts out of alignment. When we're manipulating our hearts into believing we have to be a certain way, do a certain thing, or have a certain possession, we're missing out on the treasure that is abundant life living.

Fill in the blank:

For where your treasure is, there your _____will be also. – Matthew 6:21 (NLT)

When we pretend, we lie to our hearts.

We put our treasures in what we wish we were or wish we had, and we miss out on what we do have. At what point as Jesus girls did we decide we had to have it all together to be accepted, loved, and impactful?

We're too busy pretending we're *not* broken to reach those who are.

So, how do we tear down the barrier of pretending?

For starters, we replace pretending with honesty in our own journey.

> This is a trustworthy saying, and everyone should accept it: "Christ Jesus came into the world to save sinners"—and I am the worst of them all. But God had mercy on me so that Christ Jesus could use me as a prime example of his great patience with even the worst sinners. Then others will realize that they, too, can believe in him and receive eternal life. – 1 Timothy 1:15-16 (NLT)

What do these verses say about how we can impact our own life and the life of those we encounter when we stop pretending?

_____

_____

Consider the following statements, and check the box that speaks the loudest to you:

- O I cannot expect to navigate people to Jesus when I'm walking around in full-out pretend mode day in and day out.
- O What I'm hiding behind the mask might reveal freedom to someone who is searching for a God of mercy.
- O Those who don't have it all together can find hope in seeing God work in me because I'm broken too.

Take a few minutes and reflect on the statement you checked. What do you want to say to God about this statement today? Write a brief prayer below:

_____

_____

_____

_____

_____

When we pretend, we lie to our hearts.

ENOUGH SAID: AFTER READING TODAY'S lesson, let's capture a truth and take a step in obedience.

What did you hear God specifically say to you today through His Word?

_____

_____

_____

_____

How will you respond?

_____

_____

_____

_____

A House Divided

No one can serve two masters. Either you will hate the one and love the other,
or you will be devoted to the one and despise the other.

– Matthew 6:24 (NIV)

I LIVE IN SEC COUNTRY where Saturdays down South are pretty much all we live for between late August and early December. Game day attire is planned out months in advance. Season tickets are purchased before the mortgage payment is made. And the team you represent is displayed on everything you own from your front door, to your baby's pacifier, to the license plate on your SUV.

In Arkansas, we bleed Razorback red and get the ground shakin' with our "Wooooo Pig Sooie."

And I love every minute of it.

When my husband and I met, he knew I was a Razorback fan, but I honestly think he truly fell in love when he realized I was a straight-up fanatic. He had visions in his head of watching game after game with a woman who understood first downs and could spot pass interference a mile away—it was going to be amazing enjoying the Razorbacks together.

And, then we attended our first football game.

Not only was the volume level of my passion several decibels higher than he ever anticipated, my ability to verbally share my opinion of every single play, every single player connected to the play, and the coach who called it was a little much. Let's just say it's not pretty. Or ladylike. Or attractive.

Thank you, God, that the hubs decided he could overlook this "lady in the street but a freak at the game" aspect of my personality. He just understands full well there are fair warnings that need to be given before we invite friends, family, or anyone to a game with us.

My passion runs deep.

Which explains how mystifying it is to me when I see these "house-divided" license plates, t-shirts, and home décor items complete with two teams adored by their owners. House divided? Wha?!

As for me and my house, we will Call the Hogs, and no LSU Tiger, Ole Miss Rebel or Alabama elephant or tide (whatever the heck they are) will prance in to my territory—especially my marriage and my home.

House divided. Ummmm . . . no thanks.

I cannot ring a cowbell.

I will not wear a purple and yellow t-shirt.

I refuse to sing "Rocky Top" 487 times in a three-hour time period.

I will not say "War Eagle"! Ever.

It makes me throw up in my mouth a little. I'm THAT girl. Hopelessly devoted to my Razorbacks. #NeverYield

I fully expect your emails about how much you love your Bulldogs, your Tigers, and your Volunteers. Please understand, I LOVE that you love them. Cheer them on girl! And if you see a cute outfit with a Razorback on it while trolling through your favorite online game day store, send me the link for goodness sake. I support your passion. I just can't stomach it on my person.

When I consider my commitment to people-pleasing and pretending, and my commitment to the mission God has for me, I can't help but immediately notice I'm a house divided.

On one side, I'm pushing my people-pleasing agenda with everything I have. Exhausted, empty, and overwhelmed from trying to live out the picture of perfection in my fancy-pants world.

And on the other side, I'm trying to convince myself I'm living all-in for God's agenda in my life.

I'm serving two masters. And I'm failing on both sides of this house divided.

Are you a house divided? Jot down evidence of how you are serving the people-pleasing side of your flesh and the God-centered mission in your life. (I started the list with some of my own to get you thinking.)

People-Pleasing & Pretending	God-Centered Mission
Obsessed with the next "possession" I have to have.

Spending oodles of time worrying about what others think. | Serve at Church and in my community.

Praying with coworkers. |

I love how James drops the mic on this tug-of-war of a house divided in our lives.

> But when you ask him, be sure that your faith is in **God alone.** Do not waver, for a person with divided loyalty is as unsettled as a wave of the sea that is blown and tossed by the wind. Such people should not expect to receive anything from the Lord. Their loyalty is divided between God and the world, and they are unstable in everything they do. – James 1:6-8 (NLT, emphasis mine)

In verse eight, James declares that if our loyalty is divided between God and the world, we are unstable.

Yep. That pretty much sums up my life in a nutshell.

So, how do we *stabilize* this house divided? It might be time for a good old-fashioned garage sale. Check out what Paul has to say . . .

> I once thought these things were valuable, but now I consider them worthless because of what Christ has done. Yes, everything else is worthless when compared with the infinite value of knowing Christ Jesus my Lord. For his sake I have discarded everything else, counting it all as garbage, so that I could gain Christ and become one with him. I no longer count on my own righteousness through obeying the law; rather, I become righteous through faith in Christ. For God's way of making us right with himself depends on faith. – Philippians 3:7-9 (NLT)

Can we be like Paul? Can we discard everything that's holding us back from doing what God has called us to? Can we count it all as garbage?

While I was raised on Wooooo Pig Sooie, I was also raised on certain truths that held weight in my soul. Most of these nuggets of wisdom came from my spunky, southern belle, spitfire of a "second mom"—most notably known as Aunt Jan. A cross between Thelma Harper from *Mama's Family* and Julia Sugarbaker from *Designing Women*. (Millennials: Search for these on Netflix or YouTube—you won't regret it!)

Aunt Jan was famous in our family and in pretty much any establishment she entered.

She remains a legend in these parts.

There are stories.

I would love to share them with you over coffee and a molten lava chocolate cake.

I promise we would laugh 'til we cried.

She taught me many things (all of which are not morally correct or biblical in nature), but she honed in on a few doozies I will never forget. One of those is this: One person's trash can be another's treasure.

I spent many Saturday mornings riding shot-gun in my Aunt Jan's truck trolling the garage sales in swanky-swank suburban neighborhoods all around Little Rock. We came. We conquered.

And if we weren't going to a garage sale on a spring Saturday, we were having our own.

Aunt Jan had a meticulous process for organizing her own garage sales.

1. **Inventory your junk.** And "junk" was defined as anything you have not used in the last two years (family heirlooms and those skinny jeans you might fit into one day did *not* count).
2. **Price each item.** Don't leave money on the table, but certainly don't over-price items. And add 25 cents to EVERY item. People will almost always part with an extra quarter.
3. **Tell the world about your sale.** This is where my expertise in marketing and advertising always came in handy. We might have put "OMG Becky

. . . you can't miss this sale!" on a garage sale sign. We did. It happened. I am not proud. And I warned you. There is no shame in my game.

In 2012, Aunt Jan went to be with Jesus, but I know she would love nothing more than for us to use her Garage Sale 101 outline to get rid of all that is holding us back and get busy taking on those assignments our God has for us.

1. Inventory your junk.

What is standing between where you are today and where God wants to use you?

_____

_____

_____

_____

_____

2. Price each item.

What is it costing you to hold on to the people-pleasing agenda in your house divided? Are eternities being sacrificed?

_____

_____

_____

3. Tell the world about your sale.

Have you made some significant strides in your walk with Christ, but you're holding back from sharing your growth? (Not everyone would be a fan, and the people-pleasing agenda is still reigning in your house divided.) What do you need to share with your world?

_____

_____

If our loyalty is divided between God and the world, we are unstable.

ENOUGH SAID: AFTER READING TODAY'S lesson, let's capture a truth and take a step in obedience.

What did you hear God specifically say to you today through His Word?

_____

_____

_____

_____

How will you respond?

_____

_____

_____

_____

If You Say So

You are blessed because you believed that the Lord would do what he said.

– Luke 1:45 (NLT)

FOR TWO DECADES, MY MONDAY through Fridays have been spent in the advertising and marketing business. I help brands tell their story. And my paycheck depends on if their target markets believe it. #AdAgencyLife

Advertising folks preach the mantra: perception is reality. What people, consumers, potential buyers, your target audience believes about your brand is true, whether you like it or not. When brands tell their story well, we believe them—because they say so.

I believe Southwest Airlines has the best customer service.

I believe Dunkin' Donuts has fantastic coffee.

I believe I can find anything I need in less than three clicks on Amazon.

These brand statements might not actually be true, but I believe them because they say so. And for the most part, it's been my experience that they back it up.

On the other hand . . .

I believed Milli Vanilli had singing chops. (Google it—it's fascinating!) I went to the concert. Blamed it on the rain. And bought the t-shirt.

I believed Blockbuster was the answer to my need for movie night forever and ever, amen.

I believed MySpace would be my destination of online community for decades.

They said so. But it wasn't so.

Sometimes what we believe isn't true.

34

Somewhere down the line with no advertising campaign or media strategy needed, I convinced myself people-pleasing was necessary to get what I want and where I want to go in life.

I believe the lies:

Value is in what others think of me.

If I appear to have it all together, I'll be the envy of those around me (and how can that not be fun?).

Hiding behind the mask is much better (and easier) than living out the disaster that is my life.

Broken is not beautiful. Or meaningful. Or worthy of rescue.

What lies are you believing today?

Maybe it's time to believe the truth. Focus on what God says. Bid farewell to the lies we've been believing.

> One day as Jesus was preaching on the shore of the Sea of Galilee, great crowds pressed in on him to listen to the word of God. He noticed two empty boats at the water's edge, for the fishermen had left them and were washing their nets. Stepping into one of the boats, Jesus asked Simon, its owner, to push it out into the water. So he sat in the boat and taught the crowds from there.

> When he had finished speaking, he said to Simon, "Now go out where it is deeper, and let down your nets to catch some fish."

> "Master," Simon replied, "we worked hard all last night and didn't catch a thing. But if you say so, I'll let the nets down again." And this time their nets were so full of fish they began to tear! A shout for help brought their partners in the other boat, and soon both boats were filled with fish and on the verge of sinking.

> When Simon Peter realized what had happened, he fell to his knees before Jesus and said, "Oh, Lord, please leave me—I'm such a sinful man." For he was awestruck by the number of fish they had caught, as were the others with him. His partners, James and John, the sons of Zebedee, were also amazed.

Jesus replied to Simon, "Don't be afraid! From now on you'll be fishing for people!" And as soon as they landed, they left everything and followed Jesus. – Luke 5:1-11 (NLT)

Verse five is my fav. Simon Peter gives Jesus the ol' "if you say so" reply.

We don't get the feeling Peter had much faith that those nets would fill up like they did, but because Jesus said so, the nets went back in the water.

Sometimes we have to reset our default.

Put aside past experiences and feelings and same old expectations.

We have to believe what He says.

Peter knew when he put those nets down they would come up empty again. But he did it anyway. Because Jesus said so. And after all was said and done, the men surrendered to the mission of Jesus and followed Him.

Today let's claim some truth and believe what He says.

He says His love is more than we can comprehend. Do you believe it?

And may you have the power to understand, as all God's people should, how wide, how long, how high, and how deep his love is. May you experience the love of Christ, though it is too great to understand fully. Then you will be made complete with all the fullness of life and power that comes from God. – Ephesians 3:18-19 (NLT)

He says do not be afraid. Are you?

But Moses told the people, "Don't be afraid. Just stand still and watch the Lord rescue you today." – Exodus 14:13 (NLT)

He says when we pray, He will listen. Do you believe that?

"Keep on asking, and you will receive what you ask for. Keep on seeking, and you will find. Keep on knocking, and the door will be opened to you." – Matthew 7.7 (NLT)

He says we are made new because of Jesus. Do you believe it?

This means that anyone who belongs to Christ has become a new person. The old life is gone; a new life has begun! – 2 Corinthians 5:17 (NLT)

If you believe what He says, are you ready to respond with a big "IF YOU SAY SO?"

What if we put aside the fruitless treasures of people-pleasing and pretending? Take a moment and pray for God to show you how this would impact the following areas in your life:

What do your relationships look like without people-pleasing and pretending?

_____

_____

_____

What can you accomplish when you tear down the barriers of people-pleasing and pretending and focus on God's mission for you?

_____

_____

_____

Who can you navigate to Jesus when you stop focusing on pleasing people?

_____

_____

_____

These are tough questions. Our flesh wants to rely on empty reserves of people-pleasing and pretending that have carried us through just fine thank you.

But God is begging us to believe what He says. To tear down these empty treasures and start fulfilling the purpose He has for us.

God is begging us to believe what He says.

ENOUGH SAID: AFTER READING TODAY'S lesson, let's capture a truth and take a step in obedience.

What did you hear God specifically say to you today through His Word?

_____

_____

_____

_____

How will you respond?

_____

_____

_____

_____

Oh No She Didn't

He must become greater and greater, and I must become less and less.

– John 3:30 (NLT)

YEP, IT HAPPENED. WITH LESS than a week to go before kindergarten, my five-year-old pistol of a princess decided she would take the scissors to a strand of her hair.

Lord, help me. Breathe in. Breathe out.

I know, it's funny. It really is. But that moment when I realized my child cut a chunk of hair less than an inch from her scalp, part of me collapsed. What just happened? You have GOT to be kidding me. No bow, headband, or pixie cut can make up for this tragedy.

I began chanting to myself, "Pull it together sister."

So, I did—kind of.

A decade ago, my husband would have been calling 911 (is there an emergency therapist on duty?!) and knocking on doors in the neighborhood searching for help for his deranged wife. But not on this day. Because, my perspective is shifting. I'm a work in progress.

I'm a little neurotic (cue the understatement of the year award!), a tad bit OCD, maybe slightly "wound-up," and I definitely take "type A" to the next level from time to time. But, I'm transforming—every day.

The old Priscilla would have OBSESSED over this little one's hair (or lack thereof). It would have eaten me alive, because I value people-pleasing, and living up to a certain picture of perfection for my little girl's appearance.

What about school pictures?

What will she look like?

How can I make her as perfect as possible?

Yep, I would have been overwhelmed with the shame of that haircut.

But not on this day. Something had shifted in me, if ever so slightly.

For so long, I have been overwhelmed with trying to please others and pretend I have it all together. On this day when my little munchkin decided to step in and play the role of hair stylist, I recognized that part of me had surrendered.

And it felt really good.

Instead of remaining in my obsessed state of panic over what her perfect and precious new teacher and all the other moms at school would think, I chalked it up to a memorable first-day-of-school picture that I was sure we wouldn't forget.

For you, I'm sure it's not your daughter's kindergarten hair soaking up your thoughts and energy today. (If it is, email me. We'll get through this together.) But I'm certain as we've navigated through this week of evaluating our comparison game, our pretending charade, and our eagerness to people-please you've identified some areas where you might be trapped.

The answer for our escape is Jesus.

> For I fully expect and hope that I will never be ashamed, but that I
> will continue to be bold for Christ, as I have been in the past. And
> I trust that my life will bring honor to Christ, whether I live or die.
> For to me, living means living for Christ, and dying is even better.
> But if I live, I can do more fruitful work for Christ. So I really don't
> know which is better. – Philippians 1:20 (NLT)

Consider these statements and put a check mark beside the one(s) that apply to you today.

O When my focus is on what people will think and not what He thinks, I cannot have impact.

O When I camouflage who I really am with who I think others want me to be, I can't live out loud the plan God has for me.

O When I'm obsessed with a vision of perfection I've created, I can't carry out the mission He created for me.

O When I am severed from the One True Vine, I cannot produce fruit.

I think on any given day, I fall into the truth of one (or more) of these statements.

What are you obsessing about today that might have you severed from the One True Vine?

_____

_____

_____

_____

Read John 15:1-5. Consider the phrase "Remain in me." What does that look like for you? List practical steps you can take in these areas of your life to remain in Him.

In your relationships (family, friends, other) . . .

_____

_____

_____

In your prayer life . . .

_____

_____

_____

At work (inside or outside the home) . . .

_____

_____

_____

In how you spend your time . . .

_____

_____

_____

_____

For me, fighting the battle of people-pleasing and pretending is a war within my mind. It's a conscious decision I have to make. I fight not to get caught up in the emptiness of focusing on the things that I know don't matter, and instead fixating on the value of eternity.

Paul explained it perfectly in Ephesians 4:22-24 (NIV) (fill in the blanks).

You were taught, with regard to your former way of life, to put off your _____ self, which is being corrupted by its deceitful desires; to be made _____ in the attitude of your minds; and to put on the new self, created to be like God in true righteousness and holiness.

Let's do some quick inventory. List some practices, habits, and thoughts relating to people-pleasing and pretending that need to be placed in the rear-view mirror as your "former" way of life. Then list those that need to be included in the new attitude of your mind.

Old Self (practices, habits, thoughts)   New Self (practices, habits, thoughts)

_____

_____

_____

_____

_____

_____

One of the best parts about putting our old self aside and growing in a new attitude is taking notice of our progress. And if you're like me, I think I'll ALWAYS be a work in progress.

The night my soon-to-be-kindergartner cut her hair, I felt progress in my soul. I know it probably sounds shallow. It's even a little shameful to admit it. A clip of the scissors that could have been so big in my world months earlier was a blip on my radar on this night. What I once thought was big, was now so small.

For far too long I have let people-pleasing and pretending define what is BIG in my world. As you've studied this week, what has God revealed to you that needs to be placed in the BIG and SMALL categories of your life? I've listed a couple of my own here to get you started . . .

SMALL   **BIG**

My place on the roster of the comparison game   Pretending I'm not broken

_____

_____

_____

_____

_____

_____

_____

As we wrap up this week, let's review some of the key Scriptures we've studied. Jot down what you learned from these verses this week, and put a star beside the Scripture you will commit to memory as you fight the tug-of-war between your flesh and your mission.

Romans 12:2

_____

_____

1 Timothy 1:15-16

_____

_____

Philippians 3:7-9

_____

_____

2 Corinthians 5:17

_____

_____

One of the best parts about putting our old self aside and growing in a new attitude is taking notice of our progress.

ENOUGH SAID: AFTER READING TODAY'S lesson, let's capture a truth and take a step in obedience.

What did you hear God specifically say to you today through His Word?

_____

_____

_____

How will you respond?

_____

_____

_____

I'm ready to put down the people-pleasing, comparison game-playing shenanigans we've explored this week.

Will you join me?

Let's say enough.

Enough people-pleasing.

Enough pretending.

Enough of me. More of Jesus.

Week 2:

Enough excuses. More SURRENDER.

Seek the Kingdom of God above all else, and live righteously, and he will give you everything you need.

– Matthew 6:33 (NLT)

I HAVE THIS FEAR. IT'S a classic case of claustrophobia, but it rears its head in the most surprising places. Yes, I hate to be held under the covers, be rolled into an MRI machine, or hang out in a storm shelter when the tornado sirens are blaring. But those are predictable places where it makes sense that my claustrophobia would be on full display.

You wouldn't, however, expect my claustrophobia to take over during a quick trip to my favorite shopping mall. But it did.

It was a run-in and run-out kind of visit to the mall that day. I had t-minus seventeen minutes to run in, grab a new top to wear at my speaking engagement (THAT NIGHT), and pray it fit perfectly. I had lost a few pounds and was excited to get in a smaller size. You know how you diet for three days and in your mind you've lost a significant amount of weight? I was basking in the feeling that I was even a smidge smaller than I was the last time I stepped foot in that dressing room in my favorite boutique. So, I grabbed what I thought would be the perfect size for the new me.

Bad idea.

It wasn't the tight quarters of the dressing room that got me—I'm actually surprisingly comfortable in a small dressing room. The tiny room didn't have me trapped. But the top I had selected to try on did.

As I pulled the silky blouse over my head, I immediately panicked. With bent elbows in a row-row-row-your-boat motion, I was testing the waters and realizing I was caught in this top and I may never get out.

Breathe Priscilla. You got this. You are not going to be stuck in a shirt.

Before I let my thoughts go to my Hulk-Hogan-ish skills of breaking through this blouse like a crazy woman, I tried to think rationally. I knew that if I had some help, I could get this top off with ease.

I remembered when I was a kid and I would just raise my arms up and my mom would pull off my shirt as I was changing into my pajamas or getting ready for a bath. I clung to that memory, and realized it was time to call in reinforcements.

I had heard another lady and what I thought was most likely her daughter in the dressing room beside me, so I decided to ask for help.

One problem. They didn't speak English.

By this time, I'm sweating like a wild woman, my face is bright red, and I'm on the verge of going Hulk Hogan on this top for real. The lady and her daughter were standing outside my dressing room terrified. My panic was contagious, and when I opened the door I could see the panic on their faces.

In my best charades moment to-date, I began to demonstrate to the mom how I was going to raise my hands up and then she could pull the top over my head. Yes. It was comical, and if it wasn't PG-13, I have no doubt a video of this could have gone viral and made me famous for reasons I would never wish on my worst enemy.

Despite the hilarity of the situation (no one was laughing in that dressing room hallway, by the way), my depiction of what needed to happen somehow translated to this sweet mommy-daughter duo. But, Momma wasn't going in for the save. Her daughter would be the one to save the day.

And she did.

Right there in that dressing room hallway while I was caught up in a trendy blouse one size too small, a young girl saved my dignity and a $29.99 special off the sales rack that was not meant for me. She pulled that sucker right over my head and I blurted out the loudest "Gracias" she had ever heard.

It was humiliating and exhilarating all at the same time.

Do you ever get caught up?

Ever feel trapped by something that in reality doesn't actually have you trapped at all?

My claustrophobia runs deep. It not only pops up in the dressing rooms at my favorite boutiques, but also in my explanation for not living out loud for God like I should.

I'm trapped in my excuses.

We can't accomplish the mission God has for us when we're caught up in our excuses.

And truth be told, I'm drowning some days. I have excuses for my excuses, reason after reason for why God can't use me.

Surrendering our excuses for obedience can be difficult. But we can't accomplish the mission God has for us when we're caught up in our excuses.

It's time to call in reinforcements, to dig into God's Word and see what He has to say about being trapped in the emptiness of our excuses.

Let's say enough. Let's live out our calling with abandon.

Enough excuses. More surrender.

A Cartwheel for the Win!

*For we died and were buried with Christ by baptism. And just as Christ was raised
from the dead by the glorious power of the Father, now we also may live new lives.*

– Romans 6:4 (NLT)

I DID A CARTWHEEL LAST week. And it was epic, in a "pulled a hammy"
kind of way.

My six-year-old diva of a daughter was practicing her cartwheel in our
living room, and it was the most pathetic thing I had seen on my shag rug in
a long time.

"Hand, hand, foot, foot, sister! Whip those legs around—you can do it!" I
shouted to her with encouragement in the best mom-coach voice I could dig
up after witnessing the state of her cartwheel.

Her feet were barely leaving the floor and her lack of effort was killing me.
So, without thinking it through, I stood up, tucked my shirt in, and showed
her what a real cartwheel looks like. At least I thought I did. That was certainly
my intention.

My hands did hit the floor. My legs did fly through the air. But I'm not sure
I pulled off perfection in legit cartwheel standards.

And, oh by the way, I will never be the same. Ever.

Back in the day (early 1990's if you're keeping score), I was *that* girl. The
cheerleader that could throw back-hand-springs for days on the track during
a football game. I know, it's funny. I tumbled and cheered my way through
high school, and the one thing I knew for sure was how to complete the
perfect cartwheel. So, showing my six-year-old how to do a cartwheel isn't
that crazy, is it? Maybe if it hadn't been twentyish years ago and I wasn't a
pound or two heavier.

I was not the spring chicken I thought I was in my mind. Truth be told, I hadn't even spelled the word cartwheel in two decades.

Reality check—I am not who I once was.

And neither are you.

If we're dissecting our excuses this week, I think this one sits high on our list of excuses.

God can't use me. You don't know who I am, what I've done, where I've been.

You are so right, sister. I don't know. But God does, and He couldn't care less because that girl is long gone.

> My old self has been crucified with Christ. It is no longer I who live, but Christ lives in me. So I live in this earthly body by trusting in the Son of God, who loved me and gave himself for me. I do not treat the grace of God as meaningless. For if keeping the law could make us right with God, then there was no need for Christ to die. – Galatians 2:20-21 (NLT)

We can be so caught up in who we once were. What we have done. Where we have been. The queen of spades for our deck of excuses is on full display in our minds.

God can't use me because I messed it up—big time.

Is there something in your past—from the last decade, the last year, or even last week—that is holding you back from living in the purpose God has for you? What do you need to eliminate right now, right here on these pages? Prayerfully answer these questions and bury those excuses once and for all in the space below. Write your answers and mark through them as you pray for God to remove them from your heart and mind.

_____

_____

_____

_____

Is it possible we have become professionals at making assumptions? As we're saying enough to our excuses this week, we also must take a moment and bid farewell to the theories that fuel those excuses.

List some of the assumptions that fuel your excuses here. I've started the list to help you think about what those might be for you.

I assume ...

Assumption #1: God can't use me because I'm not good enough.

Assumption #2: No one knows my past, and if they did, there is no way I could be used by God for His purpose.

Assumption #3: _____

_____

Assumption #4:_____

_____

Assumption #5:_____

_____

Now, take a few minutes and pray through these assumptions that fill your bag of excuses. Ask God to remind you that you are His masterpiece created anew. Mark through each assumption after you pray, and ask God to remove them from your mind and heart.

> For we are God's masterpiece. He has created us anew in Christ Jesus, so we
> can do the good things he planned for us long ago. – Ephesians 2:10 (NLT)

This internal battle we fight of reminding ourselves we are made new in Christ is not easy to escape.

I remember sitting on my back porch with a dear friend a few years ago. She was going through a tough time in her marriage, and she was pouring out her heart to me over a cold glass of sweet tea on a hot summer afternoon.

I will never forget her words and the picture she painted with her hands. She held her hands up as if she was holding a book, and she began to turn the pages of the book she fictitiously held.

She said, "If my life were a book and you read the pages of it, you would not be sitting here listening to me and praying with me. We would not be friends."

My heart broke for her. And, oh how wrong she was!

If you're struggling with who you once were, I will tell you like I told my dear friend on that hot summer day, the banner of the gospel we live under is powerful.

Because of Jesus we are alive in our new life in Him. That book you hold of the life you once lived has been written over and covered in grace.

Fill in the blanks:

> We know that our _____ sinful selves were crucified with Christ
> so that sin might lose its power in our lives. We are no longer slaves
> to sin. For when we died with Christ we were set _____
> from the power of sin. – Romans 6:6-7 (NLT)

Thankfully, some of us aren't held in the grips of our past sin or poor decisions; however, we are still caught up in the excuses that paralyze our mission for God's work in our lives. We're stuck in the "I'll never" excuses.

I'll never measure up.

I'll never be enough.

I'll never be what I need to be for God to use me.

We forget we are pursuing progress and not perfection.

Paul said it best in Philippians:

> I don't mean to say that I have already achieved these things or
> that I have already reached perfection. But I press on to possess
> that perfection for which Christ Jesus first possessed me. No,
> dear brothers and sisters, I have not achieved it, but I focus on
> this one thing: Forgetting the past and looking forward to what
> lies ahead, I press on to reach the end of the race and receive the
> heavenly prize for which God, through Christ Jesus, is calling
> us. – Philippians 3:12-14 (NLT)

When we surrender the pursuit of perfection and commit to progress, we're saying enough to the excuses that are holding us back from getting on mission.

What are some practical ways we can chase progress and not perfection? Add your thoughts to this list.

1. Commit to reading God's Word regularly.

2. Serve in my local church.

3.

4.

5.

Progress leads to steps of obedience that navigate people to Jesus.

Progress glorifies God in everyday moments in our cubicles, at our dinner tables, and in the line at the grocery store.

Progress matters.

We forget we are pursuing progress and not perfection.

ENOUGH SAID: AFTER READING TODAY'S lesson, let's capture a truth and take a step in obedience.

What did you hear God specifically say to you today through His Word?

_____

_____

_____

_____

How will you respond?

_____

_____

_____

_____

The Fridge List

Let us not become weary in doing good, for at the proper time we will reap a harvest if we do not give up.

– Galatians 6:9 (NLT)

I FIRMLY BELIEVE THAT MEN and women were created vastly different when it comes to our sense of urgency. Most notably when it comes to household chores, honey-dos, and the completely practical necessities of life.

Right now at this very moment, there is a list of honey-dos I have plastered on a dry erase board on my refrigerator for my husband to pass by at his leisure. It simply reads . . .

Car out of garage

Schedule college visits

Fix grill

Kennedy groomed

This to-do list seems quite reasonable to me.

O I do not want to start a junkyard in my garage. The car that currently doesn't run and sits in the garage now serves as the catch-all for "stuff we don't know where to put." #Disaster

O I would love for our senior in high school to have guidance from his dad on how/when/where to take his college visits.

O I need grilled chicken, shrimp, and a good burger in my life. Please—for the love—don't make me put one more thing in the oven this summer!

O I can't take the odor from our 16-year-old Chinese pug that hasn't had a bath in several weeks.

This list has been on the fridge for six months. *SIX. MONTHS.*

Couple of things before you get ready to hit send on that email to me:

I know my seventeen-year-old should schedule his own college visits. But there are days he forgets to brush his teeth, so I'm not super-comfortable leaving this completely up to him at this point. #CutMeSomeSlack

And, yes, I have the ability to pick up the phone and schedule an appointment with our dog-groomer, or better yet, give our dog, Kennedy, a bath myself. But I know it's not gonna happen. I am a wanna-be dog person with a dog. #PrayForKennedy

In the hubs' defense, he handles *a lot* of the household duties and is a true rock star in the game of life. If I cook, he cleans the kitchen. He is obsessed with the yard and all that is edging, blowing, and living up to the neighborhood standards of what our yard should look like. While I juggle work, family, and ministry and all that entails, he helps check homework, crafts his best ponytails for the youngest of our clan, and keeps us all in check as we chase after all of the things that matter and don't in our crazy life at Camp Peters. And, oh by the way, he works outside the home and serves in ministry, too.

He is amazing. And, he has a name – it's Coby. #LoveYouMeanItBabe

While he is the love of my life, it is evident his priorities are not mine. The projects, tasks, and responsibilities I need him to conquer in my type-A mindset are not necessarily important to him. Clearly this is not the season to ask for the car to be towed to the junk yard . . . college visits to be scheduled . . . a grilled steak . . . or a grooming appointment for my senior citizen puppy. I get it. If I want these things done, I'll have to assist or better yet do it myself.

So, the seventeen-year-old and I are heading to college visit number one in two weeks, and the dog is getting groomed on Saturday. I don't have the patience or the bandwidth to tackle the car or the grill. So, I'll just sit back and wait on those as patiently as possible. Ahem . . . ok, I'll try.

Before this quickly turns into a marriage counseling session for me, my control issues, and my need to "get it done now, please!" I think we can analyze this list on my fridge from a different viewpoint.

While I'm pointing out the honey-do list on my fridge that my better half is a pro at ignoring, if I'm honest, I have a list I've been ignoring too.

God has given me a list of next steps—a list of assignments—tasks I'm called to complete.

I wish I could say the list has been on the fridge for only six months.

I hear the leading, directing, and guiding in my heart to take on people, projects, and mission. But I always grab at one of my favorite excuses in my bag of reasons why I can't finish the work God has for me.

This isn't the right season.

We can all fill in the blanks with these excuses that loom in our minds.

This isn't my season to serve. I'm working on my _____
(fill in the blank – marriage, family, career, etc.)

It's not the right time to invite my friend to Church. It's _____
(fill in the blank – baseball season, football season, summer and time for us to be at the lake every weekend, etc.)

I'm still praying about that, so I'm not ready to commit to _____
(fill in the blank – taking that leadership role, sharing my faith with my coworker, starting a bible study with my friends/coworkers, etc.)

Sometimes we fall on the crutch of seasons in our life to distract us from finishing the work God has put in front of us.

Read Ruth Chapter 1.

In this passage, Ruth finds herself in a difficult season. In the first few verses, we learn that her father-in-law, her husband, and her brother-in-law have all passed away, and she is left in Moab with her mother-in-law, Naomi, and her sister-in-law, Orpah.

Naomi was heading back to her homeland of Judah, so Ruth and Orpah were getting ready to leave and return to their homeland and be separated from Naomi. The three of them wept as they planned to set out on a path back to their families.

But something stirred in Ruth's heart. She couldn't leave Naomi and the God she had encountered. She couldn't turn her back on God and the plan she must have sensed He had for her.

> And again they wept together, and Orpah kissed her mother-in-law good-bye. But Ruth clung tightly to Naomi. "Look," Naomi said to her, "your sister-in-law has gone back to her people and to her gods. You should do the same."

> But Ruth replied, "Don't ask me to leave you and turn back. Wherever you go, I will go; wherever you live, I will live. Your people will be my people, and your God will be my God. Wherever you die, I will die, and there I will be buried. May the Lord punish me severely if I allow anything but death to separate us!" When Naomi saw that Ruth was determined to go with her, she said nothing more. – Ruth 1:14-18 (NLT)

As we read on in Ruth, she continues to follow the direction and mission God puts in front of her, and her commitment to God and His mission points to a generational line leading all the way to David and beyond.

Ruth could have easily gone back to her family and missed out on all God had for her and a generational legacy that ultimately changed the world.

She didn't get caught up in the excuse of her season, or the timing, or her own expectations for how the story might unfold. She was faithful and obedient with the mission God put in front of her. She responded to the tug on her heart.

I'm certain God is tugging on our hearts. If not today, then yesterday, last week, or last year. But, I'm confident we have a to-do list from Him. Tasks to complete. Assignments to fulfill. People to share with, love on, and encourage.

What has God put on your fridge list? Why is that list incomplete? Use the space below to jot down your answers.

TASKS/ASSIGNMENTS/PEOPLE   REASON/EXCUSE IT'S INCOMPLETE

_____

_____

_____

_____

_____

_____

When we surrender our excuses and trade them in for obedience, the work begins and the harvest is gathered. Are you blaming your paralysis in mission on your current season? Because, if we're waiting for everything to be just right before we finish the work, we're missing the bounty in the fields—right now.

> Then Jesus explained: "My nourishment comes from doing the will of God, who sent me, and from finishing his work. You know the saying, 'Four months between planting and harvest.' But I say, wake up and look around. The fields are already ripe for harvest.
> – John 4:34-35 (NLT)

It's time to surrender our seasons—to say enough to the excuses that lead us to believe that mission can wait.

The time is always right for God to work. The mission of making disciples cannot wait.

Enough excuses.

When we surrender our excuses and trade them in for obedience, the work begins and the harvest is gathered.

ENOUGH SAID: AFTER READING TODAY'S lesson, let's capture a truth and take a step in obedience.

What did you hear God specifically say to you today through His Word?

_____

_____

_____

_____

How will you respond?

_____

_____

_____

_____

The "J" Word

If you are faithful in little things, you will be faithful in large ones. But if you are dishonest in little things, you won't be honest with greater responsibilities.

– Luke 16:10 (NLT)

I HAVE A FEW PET peeves. Those little things in life that bug you to death. They seep inside your soul and aggravate every part of your being. Yep. *THOSE* things.

One of these little nuggets of life happens often at work, and it's rooted in one word. In fact, it IS a word. The word is JUST.

Not the word "just" in the "fair, impartial, objective" kind of way. But "just" in the "only, merely, simple" kind of way.

Hang with me here for a minute, and I'm certain this will make perfect sense.

As I mentioned last week, I work in the advertising and marketing business. So, I'm constantly getting projects thrown at me that range from writing a blog post, to creating a presentation for a colleague, drafting a Request for Proposal (RFP) response for a potential client, coordinating events, drafting social media content, and so on. These projects vary in the level of time, effort, and resources that are required to complete the task, but they all take up square feet on any marketer's to-do list.

Marketing and advertising gurus wear many hats. We typically love them all. But, don't throw a "just" in the mix. EVER.

It's *just* a blog post.

All I need is a presentation. It's *just* a PowerPoint.

We did an RFP last month, so for this one, you'll *just* have to copy and paste the answers (to completely different questions from a completely different company?).

Let's *just* do a webinar for that.

When I hear the word "just" in these situations, what I'm really hearing is a lack in value of the work. It's not a big deal. It's easy. It doesn't matter.

In my colleagues' defense, I've dropped a "j" bomb or two myself. I might have told a web developer, "it's *just* a landing page," and said to a graphic designer, "it's *just* a magazine ad." #Guilty

The sting of this word that minimizes and belittles the work before it's even done overshadows the work itself.

An assignment seems insignificant and inconsequential when we paint it in this light of unworthy and therefore inconsequential.

Which leads us back to digging into our bag of excuses.

We throw a "just" on some of the most powerful assignments and tasks God calls us to, and in some cases we ignore them because they're not big enough, awesome enough, or perfect enough.

I guess I'll "just" pray about it. There's nothing else I can do.

I "just" have fifteen minutes in the morning, that's not enough time to really get into God's Word.

We can't have children, so we're "just" going to adopt or foster.

Our "just" is getting in the way of God's purpose in our lives. How can we finish the work God's called us to if we are somehow minimizing the assignments He has for us?

In Matthew chapter nine, Jesus has a brief encounter with a woman who doesn't allow her "just" to be an excuse. In fact, she leans in and flips the script on the "j" word. She knows if she can "just" get close enough to touch his robe, she might be changed forever. And she is.

> Just then a woman who had suffered for twelve years with constant bleeding came up behind him. She touched the fringe of his robe, for she thought, "If I can just touch his robe, I will be healed."

Jesus turned around, and when he saw her he said, "Daughter, be encouraged! Your faith has made you well." And the woman was healed at that moment. – Matthew 9:20-22 (NLT)

How can we follow this woman's lead, flip the script on our "just," and turn what we once saw as meaningless God assignments into meaningful life change for us and those around us?

What mission or God assignment has God put on your heart, but you've never followed through because you thought it was too insignificant or unimportant?

_____

_____

_____

_____

What lofty mission has God put on your heart, but you haven't moved forward because you believe it's "just" too big for you?

_____

_____

_____

_____

List some of your common "just" excuses that keep you from fulfilling God's mission in your life.

1. I don't want to _____, it's "just" not a big deal.
2. It's okay if I don't _____, because I "just" don't have time during this season in my life.

(Fill in the blank with another "just" excuse that creeps up often in your life): _____

_____

Over the past four or five years, I've been praying simple prayers of surrender. I've been asking God to show me what surrender looks like in my life, so I can take practical steps to live with abandon in the calling He has on my life.

I have seen amazing fruit from these prayers. This Bible Study is a result of those prayers. What started as a few simple tugs on my heart resulted in full out, on-my-knees, tear-filled face-plants of surrender. When I lay down my excuses, I've never felt more alive and on mission.

When our hearts are saturated with a desire, a calling, a nudge to take a step of faith and unleash surrender, we can't let our excuse that it's not enough or it's way too much get in the way. When God gives us that push, the time is "just" right.

> Let the morning bring me word of your unfailing love, for I have put my trust in you.
>
> Show me the way I should go, for to you I entrust my life. Rescue me from my enemies, Lord, for I hide myself in you. Teach me to do your will, for you are my God; may your good Spirit lead me on level ground. – Psalm 143:8-10 (NIV)

As you read these words today, what does bold surrender look like in your life? What is God calling you to surrender and entrust in Him today?

_____

_____

_____

_____

Today's questions might seem heavy, and big, and maybe even a little overwhelming. Saying enough is challenging. But let's not get caught up in the "j" word.

Enough excuses. More surrender.

When I lay down my excuses, I've never felt more alive and on mission.

ENOUGH SAID: AFTER READING TODAY'S lesson, let's capture a truth and take a step in obedience.

What did you hear God specifically say to you today through His Word?

_____

_____

_____

_____

How will you respond?

_____

_____

_____

_____

Newsflash: You Have a Calling

Therefore I, a prisoner for serving the Lord, beg you to lead a life worthy of your calling, for you have been called by God.

– Ephesians 4:1 (NLT)

YOU ARE CALLED BY GOD.

I know that sounds heavy and official and maybe a little weird, but it's true. You are called.

We typically hold this "calling" for preachers, missionaries, and ministry leaders of all kinds. But, you, my sister, are called by God.

The single mom digging deep every day to make ends meet and be the mom you want to be. You are called.

The career woman climbing that corporate ladder with everything you have. You are called.

The mom who lives life carpooling kiddos, wiping runny noses, and just trying to see life over the pile of laundry that awaits. You are called.

The unattached woman at any age longing for a partner in crime to share life with, or content and happy right where you are in your singlehood. You are called.

No matter where you are today, if you have a relationship with Jesus, you are called to do His work.

Our bag of excuses can easily drum up one of my favorite go-to reasons to be happy just where I am thank you very much. God can't use me. I don't have those "gifts" others have. I can't speak or write or lead. I'm not a Bible scholar. I have no idea how to organize a ministry. I just don't have it in me.

Can you pray?

Can you change a diaper and rock a baby?

Can you bake a cake or a casserole like nobody's business?

Can you listen?

Can you invite someone to Church?

Can you encourage your coworkers?

God can use you.

I love the story of Rahab in Joshua 2. It's a beautiful picture of how God can use us for His glory, even in the midst of our brokenness.

Read Joshua 2:1-8

Moses has just died, and Joshua is the new leader of the Israelites. One of his first acts as their leader was sending out two spies to scout out the land around Jericho. So, the spies headed out and ended up at the house of a prostitute named Rahab.

The King of Jericho received word that the spies were there, so he sent his messengers to Rahab's house to capture them. When they arrived, Rahab told them they had been there, but had left and she didn't know who they were. She sent the king's men away with instructions to look for them outside the city gates, while they were in fact hiding on her roof.

> "I know the Lord has given you this land," she told them. "We are all afraid of you. Everyone in the land is living in terror. For we have heard how the Lord made a dry path for you through the Red Sea when you left Egypt. And we know what you did to Sihon and Og, the two Amorite kings east of the Jordan River, whose people you completely destroyed. No wonder our hearts have melted in fear! No one has the courage to fight after hearing such things. For the Lord your God is the supreme God of the heavens above and the earth below.

> "Now swear to me by the Lord that you will be kind to me and my family since I have helped you." – Joshua 2:9-12 (NLT)

Rahab recognized who God was. She understood His goodness and wanted to be a part of His purpose. She didn't let the fact that she was a prostitute hold her back from taking part in the mission of protecting the men God had sent her way.

She didn't say, "God can't use me. I'm a prostitute! How could I possibly play a part?" Nope—she knew she had a place in this story, she sent those men to her roof for protection, and in turn, she was risking everything.

For Rahab it was two spies from the Israelite camp. But, who or what has God sent you?

In the space below, describe a time when God sent you a specific situation to live out your calling.

_____

_____

_____

_____

Take a few minutes and think about the places God has you today and the people or circumstances He has sent you. What opportunities do you have today to step into the calling God has on your life?

_____

_____

_____

_____

Now, think about what is holding back? Are you reluctant or uneasy about who or what God has sent you? Jot down your thoughts here.

_____

_____

_____

_____

Sometimes I overcomplicate this calling, and my gut tells me that maybe you do too. I'm searching for the billboard of life that's flashing with bright lights with my calling plastered on it with the mightiest of bells and whistles. And, instead, this calling shows up in the simplest ways in my everyday existence.

> "You are the light of the world—like a city on a hilltop that cannot be hidden. No one lights a lamp and then puts it under a basket. Instead, a lamp is placed on a stand, where it gives light to everyone in the house. In the same way, let your good deeds shine out for all to see, so that everyone will praise your heavenly Father."
> – Matthew 5:14-16 (NLT)

We are called to be the light in this dark world, and most of the time it doesn't require anything flashy or over-the-top in any form or fashion.

When a friend pours out her heart to me about how she's struggling in her divorce, and I walk her through the promises in Isaiah 43, reminding her that when we go through deep waters, God is with us it's a calling to be the light.

When I hear the mom in front of me in line for pictures with Santa tell Santa's Helper she can't afford a package with pictures, but she wants her kids to have the experience, and I know I have an extra twenty dollar bill—it's a calling to be the light.

When I'm compelled to encourage Sean, the guy who packs my online grocery order in my car every Friday—it's a calling to be the light.

> I pray that your hearts will be flooded with light so that you can understand the confident hope he has given to those he called—his holy people who are his rich and glorious inheritance.
> – Ephesians 1:18 (NLT)

Today, let's surrender these excuses. Draw a line through each of the lies below that you carry in your bag of excuses.

○ ~~I have no gifts – God can't use me.~~
○ I have no opportunities for God to use me.
○ I don't really have a calling, God hasn't given me a sign.

○ God can't use me because of my past. I'm too broken.

○ (Fill in the blank with another lie you're carrying in your bag of excuses.)_____

Every single day you are called. I am called. When we say enough to the excuse that God can't use us, we surrender those excuses and the light of the world shines through us.

Let's surrender our everyday routine and revive it in the calling on our lives.

Enough excuses. More surrender.

let's surrender our everyday routine and revive it in the calling on our lives.

ENOUGH SAID: AFTER READING TODAY'S lesson, let's capture a truth and take a step in obedience.

What did you hear God specifically say to you today through His Word?

_____

_____

_____

_____

How will you respond?

_____

_____

_____

_____

Captain Obvious

Since we are living by the Spirit, let us follow the Spirit's leading in every part of our lives.

– Galatians 5:25 (NLT)

I AM CAPTAIN OBVIOUS.

I'm certain it drives my family and coworkers crazy. It's a curse and a blessing all the same. The need for crystal clarity in all things is an obsession I wear daily.

When I travel for work, I leave my husband a rundown of the days I'm gone. While I know he appreciates the notes about the schedule highlighting where kiddos need to be on what day, I'm not sure he appreciates the obvious. I feel the need to remind him to pack my daughter a lunch for school. He rolls his eyes every time, but in my defense I have received a phone call from the teacher that my daughter had an empty lunchbox. So, a reminder to pack a lunch will always be a part of my rundown.

As a daughter of Christ, this identity of Captain Obvious poses issues for me. My need for black and white, yes or no, all or nothing, makes it difficult to wade through the nuances of God's Word and discern exactly what the Spirit is saying to me.

The bag of excuses we've been wading through this week has me gripped in this same conundrum. Often the excuses standing between where I am today and where God wants to use me are subtle, quiet, and hard to identify. They seep into my routine and don't call themselves out as obvious.

> Therefore, since we are surrounded by such a huge crowd of witnesses to the life of faith, let us strip off every weight that slows us down, especially the sin that so easily trips us up. And let us run

72

with endurance the race God has set before us. We do this by keeping our eyes on Jesus, the champion who initiates and perfects our faith. Because of the joy awaiting him, he endured the cross, disregarding its shame. Now he is seated in the place of honor beside God's throne.
– Hebrews 12:1-2 (NLT)

I've read these verses several times, and I've always focused on the obvious. In verse one, Paul says strip off everything slowing us down, especially sin. Honestly, when I've studied these verses, I've always focused on the sin that is holding me back, and rightfully so. But recently, I found the word "especially" buried in this gem of a message for me.

The author of Hebrews didn't say *only* focus on the sin that is holding us back, but *especially* sin.

Excuses are heavy. When we carry them, they have the ability to bring us to a complete stand still.

Some of the obvious barriers holding us back from getting on mission for God might be sin, but what about everything else? I think our bag of excuses falls in this other category of weight that is slowing us down.

Let's take a moment and do some inventory. List some of the sin in your life that is slowing you down. And, then list any excuses you're holding on to that stand between where you are today and where God can use you.

SIN   **EXCUSES**

_____

_____

_____

_____

As we wrap up this week of saying enough to the excuses that are holding us back from getting on mission, I think we would be amiss if we left out another obvious obstacle in our battle of throwing away the excuses we're carrying. And while I hate to give our enemy much square feet in a study of God's Word, I think the battle he forges in us against our mission is clear.

> We are human, but we don't wage war as humans do. We use God's mighty weapons, not worldly weapons, to knock down the strongholds of human reasoning and to destroy false arguments.
> – 2 Corinthians 10:3-4 (NLT)

Our excuses are the enemy's weapon, but the Holy Spirit can conquer any human reasoning and false argument.

Read Ephesians 6:13-18.

How can you use the Armor of God against the excuses the enemy uses as weapons in our lives? Provide an answer in the blanks below.

The Belt of Truth _____

_____

The Breastplate of Righteousness_____

_____

The Shoes of Peace _____

_____

The Shield of Faith _____

_____

The Helmet of Salvation _____

_____

The Sword of the Spirit (the Word of God) _____

_____

When we hear the enemy say God can't use me, because of my past, let's put on the helmet of salvation.

When we are buried in the excuse of "I'm too busy," let's put on the shoes of peace, and walk out of the chaos of chasing emptiness.

When we feel alone and lost, convinced we're never going to be enough for God to work in our lives, let's cling to the sword of the spirit, the mighty Word of God and let His truth breathe light into those dark places.

Our excuses have held us back for far too long. It's time to surrender our excuses for obedience in our calling.

When we hold tight to our bag of excuses, we're a threat to eternities.

> By God's grace and mighty power, I have been given the privilege of serving him by spreading this Good News. Though I am the least deserving of all God's people, he graciously gave me the privilege of telling the Gentiles about the endless treasures available to them in Christ. – Ephesians 3:7-8 (NLT)

When I surrender my excuses, I'm rescuing my mission.

It might sound bold, scary, and a little in-your-face that our excuses could hold the weight of eternities, but consider the impact our grip on our excuses can have on the people we encounter in our journey.

As we wrap up this week, let's recap the impact exchanging our excuses for more surrender has on our lives and the lives of those around us.

Let's surrender the pursuit of perfection and commit to progress.

Let's trade our excuses for surrender in every season.

Let's lay down our excuses and allow mission to come alive in our hearts.

Let's shake-up our every routine and live out our calling.

Enough excuses. More surrender.

Our excuses are the enemy's weapon, but the Holy Spirit can conquer any human reasoning and false argument

ENOUGH SAID: AFTER READING TODAY'S lesson, let's capture a truth and take a step in obedience.

What did you hear God specifically say to you today through His Word?

_____

_____

_____

_____

How will you respond?

_____

_____

_____

_____

Let's say enough and destroy every excuse we're carrying.

Are you with me?

Enough excuses. More surrender.

Enough of me. More of Jesus.

Week 3:

Enough *anxiety.* More PEACE.

I am leaving you with a gift—peace of mind and heart. And the peace I give is a gift the world cannot give. So don't be troubled or afraid.

– John 14:27 (NLT)

I'M AN EXPERT WHEN IT comes to choosing a restaurant. I've got the Open Table points and the thighs to prove it.

I'm not necessarily a "foodie," but more a lazy mom who has a tribe to feed and lacks the energy to call on my inner Rachael Ray to pull it together. I've learned that when my family is "hangry" take-out or dine-in do the trick quicker than me in the kitchen at Camp Peters.

When the family is ready to eat—you better nail down the decision of where to go—fast. So, I've perfected the art of "name that restaurant."

Side note: this DOES NOT apply to date nights with the hubs. Divorce attorneys have been on speed dial in the date-night choosing of the eating establishment. So let's not go there. Y'all—it's a thing!

Much like my crew of misfits, I bet you get "hangry" too.

I have the privilege of serving in women's ministry, and as a result, I get to listen and observe women in all seasons of life. One common thread, regardless of the season, is that we're "hangry" for peace. Real peace.

We're exhausted.

Overwhelmed.

Worried.

Broken and messed up.

We're behind, and it's too late.

We're juggling too much and dropping everything.

We need peace. We long for peace.

> Then Jesus said, "Come to me, all of you who are weary and carry heavy burdens, and I will give you rest. Take my yoke upon you. Let me teach you, because I am humble and gentle at heart, and you will find rest for your souls. – Matthew 11:28-29 (NLT)

Oh, how we long for this rest for our souls.

If you're "hangry" for peace, the restaurant is always open, and the Head Chef remains on His throne.

No reservation needed.

Your table is waiting.

Jesus picked up the tab.

Imagine what life would look like if our "hanger" for peace was fulfilled.

Nights would be full of sleep and not insomnia.

Medicine cabinets would be less full.

Tempers would not flare as often.

Panic attacks would cease.

Palms would become less sweaty.

Fewer donuts might be consumed.

When we say enough to the anxiety that is rocking our world, we let the peace of God into the cracks of our life that are begging for peace-filled, living water.

If our appetite for peace was fulfilled, I believe we might begin to breathe. Really breathe.

When we concluded last week, we highlighted how the Armor of God can be used to tear down the excuses that are holding us back from getting on mission for God. One of the pieces of that armor are the shoes of peace. His peace is both a weapon and comfort for us, and we can't even begin to understand what our lives can be when the peace of God guards our hearts and minds.

This week, we're going to unwrap what that peace looks like in our lives. When we say enough to the anxiety that is rocking our world, we let the peace of God into the cracks of our life that are begging for peace-filled, living water.

I'm beyond "hangry" for this peace. And, chances are you are too. Letting go of the anxiety that has had its grips on our hearts and minds for so long is tough. But, I believe God has so much more for us than sleepless nights, panic-filled minds, and anxiety-ridden lives. When our hearts are filled with his peace, we can live out His calling on our lives with peace-filled abandon.

We cannot finish the work God has called us to of glorifying him and navigating people to Jesus when we're wrapped up in anxiety and pursuing everything that brings on even more. It's high time we say enough to the anxiety that's ruling our lives.

Enough worry.

Enough control.

Enough stress.

Enough anxiety. More peace.

The Worry Train Departed at the DMV

The Lord gives his people strength. The Lord blesses them with peace.

– Psalm 29:11 (NLT)

I'M A WORRYWART AT HEART. If I was paid to worry, I'd be filthy rich.

What about you? Are you on the mind train to Worryville and can't seem to get the train off the tracks?

Many days, worry consumes me. Every single bit of me. Looking back, it's been this way since my teenage years.

I am the product of a blended family. My parents had four kids in their very own "his, mine, and ours" circus. They juggled us kids, a business, serving in the church, and I'm pretty sure my mom volunteered for anything and everything—she just could not say no. So, as a teenager, when I scored my driver's license, I also found my first real taste of independence.

At the Shrader house, when you received your driver's license, it wasn't necessarily a celebration, because you were officially independent of any parental chaperone unless it was an emergency. Trips to the grocery store, doctor appointments (except those of the serious nature), school, any engagement that didn't require a parent we were on our own once we could drive ourselves. For me, this independence came with both confidence and fear. I love that my parents forced us to become grown-ups in the practical areas of life. It served me well in my early adult years.

For the most part, adulting came easy and I adjusted well, except at the DMV.

The first real anxiety I remember having in my life was when I had to go to the DMV alone as a teenager. I had a new car, and it was time to get my car registered and get the required tags for the vehicle. I had been with my mom

81

to the DMV previously, and I knew it was a thing. Long lines, questions about paperwork, frustration reigned at the DMV, and I knew I wanted no part of it.

My mom assured me I had all the required paperwork. She walked me through the process of assessing the vehicle (in Arkansas we have Personal Property Taxes—Yippee!). Then, she explained to me the paperwork the DMV representative would need to get my new vehicle registered. She prepared me well.

The night before I planned on going, I couldn't sleep. I was imagining how everything would go wrong. I was literally sick to my stomach. It's the first time I remember worry truly taking over my heart and my mind. My trip to the DMV turned out fine. Although, when I first walked in, I didn't take a number. And, we all know that is not a good start for your DMV experience.

More often than not, my anxiety manifests itself through worry in my life. Over the years, worry over trivial trips to the DMV have been replaced with worry over anything I cannot control. Since those teenage years, I've fought the battle of worry in my heart and mind almost daily.

Worry at work.

Worry at home.

Worry about my family.

Worry about what others think of me.

Worry over my finances.

Worry about having so much to do and so little time.

Worry over living up to what my mom and dad expect of me, even as an adult.

Worry I'm not going to say the right thing.

Worry I'm going to be too much or not enough.

It's a runaway train of worry that leads to overwhelming anxiety.

Can you relate? Take a minute and write down some areas in your life where worry floods in consistently.

_____

_____

_____

_____

God's Word is clear on how we should handle the anxiety that comes from worry in our lives.

> Don't worry about anything; instead, pray about everything. Tell God what you need, and thank him for all he has done. Then you will experience God's peace, which exceeds anything we can understand. His peace will guard your hearts and minds as you live in Christ Jesus. – Philippians 4:6-7 (NLT)

The peace of God stops our runaway mind train in its tracks. We just have to call on it. We have to replace worry with prayer, thanksgiving, and appeals to God of what we need.

Take the list you made earlier of areas in your life where you're worrying today, and replace that worry with prayer for what you need and thanksgiving for what God has already provided.

My Worry	My Prayer for This Worry	What I'm Thankful For

Read 2 Chronicles 20.

King Jehoshaphat had plenty to worry about. Armies were marching for him and his people ready to declare war. He was terrified, but instead of worry getting a grip on him, he called out to the Lord.

"O our God, won't you stop them? We are powerless against this mighty army that is about to attack us. We do not know what to do, but we are looking to you for help." – 2 Chronicles 20:12 (NLT)

He prayed. He literally bowed down before the Lord. And, God rescued him and his people. The armies declaring war on his people began fighting against themselves, and Jehoshaphat and his people were not afraid or discouraged. They trusted God.

So Jehoshaphat's kingdom was at peace, for his God had given him rest on every side. – 2 Chronicles 20:30 (NLT)

Jehoshaphat knew God would fight his battle. He swapped his worry out for trust, and the battle was won before it really even began.

It's impossible to get on mission when our lives are saturated with worry, and we're not asking and trusting God in the rescue.

Worry can be a barrier to mission in our lives. Is there anything you're worried about today that is standing in the way of you taking a step in obedience?

_____

_____

_____

_____

As we wrap up today, pray through the worry that has a grip on you. Ask God to fill the gaps with His favor and His peace.

Let's say enough to the anxiety caused by the worry in our lives.
Enough worrying. More peace.

The peace of God stops our runaway mind train in its tracks.

ENOUGH SAID: AFTER READING TODAY'S lesson, let's capture a truth and take a step in obedience.

What did you hear God specifically say to you today through His Word?

_____

_____

_____

_____

How will you respond?

_____

_____

_____

_____

Control Freaks Anonymous

So I say, let the Holy Spirit guide your lives. Then you won't be doing what your sinful nature craves.

– Galatians 5:16 (NLT)

HELLO, MY NAME IS PRISCILLA. And I'm a control freak. The real, legit, control freak of nature that Type B's despise and husbands run as fast as they can from—I'm her. Thankfully, my family and close friends respond to my control freakiness with baskets full of grace. My heart is so grateful.

The need to control every human being around me, every situation I'm smack dab in the middle of, and any project I'm assigned to is just the beginning. My control issues run deep, and so does the anxiety that rides the coattails of my need to be in control of all things thank you very much.

Whether you're with me in the need to start our own Control Freaks Anonymous group, or you struggle slightly with control issues, we could all use a dose of surrender from time to time. Because surrender produces peace when control has its tight grip.

Today, let's look at a brief encounter the people of Gadarenes had with Jesus and see if we can relate.

> When Jesus arrived on the other side of the lake, in the region of the Gadarenes, two men who were possessed by demons met him. They came out of the tombs and were so violent that no one could go through that area.
>
> They began screaming at him, "Why are you interfering with us, Son of God? Have you come here to torture us before God's appointed time?"

There happened to be a large herd of pigs feeding in the distance. So the demons begged, "If you cast us out, send us into that herd of pigs."

"All right, go!" Jesus commanded them. So the demons came out of the men and entered the pigs, and the whole herd plunged down the steep hillside into the lake and drowned in the water.

The herdsmen fled to the nearby town, telling everyone what happened to the demon-possessed men. Then the entire town came out to meet Jesus, but they begged him to go away and leave them alone. – Matthew 8:28-34 (NLT)

Verse thirty-four says the people of the town begged him to go away and leave them alone.

The anxiety that manifests in our hearts from the control we want on our lives begs Jesus to go away.

We're basically saying, "You can leave me alone. I'm good."

I mean, I go to church. So, we'll just keep You right there, and I'll be mighty fine checking in on Sundays and maybe a Wednesday night here and there. But, these everyday moments—I got them.

Holding Jesus close can be impossible, if we're not allowing Him to invade our to-do lists, our calendars, and our fleshly agendas in our day-to-day moments of life. We're in control and we're holding Him at a distance in case He creeps in and does something whacky, unimaginable, or downright crazy.

This relationship with Jesus that we walked into and put our hearts on the line for didn't include a contract that said we would drive the bus and allow Jesus to take a ride every now and then—on our terms.

Our relationship with Jesus should invade every ounce of our lives. We should be handing Him the keys to the bus, forfeiting our GPS, the steering wheel, and the cup holder at the front of the bus. He's the driver. And when we become a passenger and let Him drive, He will take us where we never dreamed or imagined we could go.

Take a few minutes and think about these two equations:

My Life + My Control = Anxiety   My Life + Jesus = Peace

In what areas of your life do you have the most anxiety?

_____

_____

_____

_____

_____

Perform a quick audit on these areas of your life. Are you fighting for control, and is it time to surrender these areas to God so you can walk in peace? Prayerfully consider each area you listed above that produces anxiety in your life today. What practical steps can you take to surrender them?

Life Area	Are You In Control? (Y/N)	Step I Can Take in Surrender

Control is like a drug. The more we have, the more we want. The need for control produces anxiety, and when we're overcome with anxiety, it's difficult for God to do a work in us and through us.

James gives us a warning about control.

Now listen, you who say, "Today or tomorrow we will go to this or that city, spend a year there, carry on business and make money." Why, you do not even know what will happen tomorrow. What is your life? You are a mist that appears for a little while and then vanishes. Instead, you ought to say, "If it is the Lord's will, we will live and do this or that." As it is, you boast in your arrogant schemes. All such boasting is evil. – James 4:13-16 (NIV)

Arrogant schemes? But, Lord, I'm just a planner. A girl with a mission for perfection in my mile long to-do list. I know where I need to be, who I need to be with, what I need to wear, and how long it's going to take. Right?

Wrong sister.

The arrogance of my flesh begs for control, and when I find myself in the mess of life, I call out to God, "Where are You?"

"Right here dear one. I'm right here," He says.

"You've been too busy chasing your own agenda that you have completely neglected Mine."

Today as we wrap up, let's surrender control so we can find peace outside our anxiety.

Before you carry on with your day, pray a prayer of surrender over the areas of your life that you listed on the previous page.

Let's say enough to the anxiety produced by the tight grip of control we have on our lives.

Enough control. More peace.

The need for control produces anxiety, and when we're overcome with anxiety, it's difficult for God to do a work in us and through us.

ENOUGH SAID: AFTER READING TODAY'S lesson, let's capture a truth and take a step in obedience.

What did you hear God specifically say to you today through His Word?

_____

_____

_____

_____

How will you respond?

_____

_____

_____

_____

Suck it Up Sister

Give all your worries and cares to God, for he cares about you.

– 1 Peter 5:7 (NLT)

IT WAS A HOT SUMMER day in Arkansas when the humidity was so thick you're hair had no hope and sweat rolled down every part of your being. I was ten years old, so I didn't care.

It was my very first softball game. I had never played a game, but had begged my dad to sponsor a team. Wearing my Shrader Construction uniform with pride, I showed up to the game a half hour early like my coach had instructed.

We were warming up, and I was playing second base. I had no business even being on the field, much less playing second base, but my Dad was sponsoring the team, so I'm sure the coaches felt compelled to add me to the line-up. As our coach hit us balls for the warm up, I was holding my own, but then he shot a few pop flies through the air for each infielder to take. Lord help me.

When my turn rolled around, the ball soared straight up in the air above me, and I yelled "I got it!" as if someone else was going to catch my practice pop fly.

I'm not sure my glove even got close to the ball, because all I can remember is the ball nailing me right smack dab in the middle of my face. Blood went everywhere. I dropped my glove, and with tears streaming down my face ran to my dad in horror wondering if I had broken my nose and if I would ever look the same.

Dad was holding back his laughter, and simply said, "Suck it up."

Ummmmm . . . your little girl has just taken a ball to the nose, I'm going to need a little bit of sympathy here.

"Suck it up. Wash your face off, and get back out there," Dad said. Shraders are no quitters.

So, I spent the remainder of the season in right field playing with the flowers praying no ball would ever come my way, and retired my softball glove after that one season. #NeverAgain

God is pretty clear in His Word that life is going to get rough. We will be smacked in the face with struggles, suffering, grief, and hardships. It's a guarantee. (Romans 5:3 | James 1:2-4 | 1 Peter 1:6)

Anxiety no doubt comes with those fly balls of life that hit us smack in the face. If we're not careful, the anxiety that comes from the trials and struggles of this world can paralyze us in our mission and purpose.

I don't know about you, but my conversations with my Heavenly Father are typically blunt and candid in nature. Sometimes, He echoes the voice of my dad here on Earth, and I hear Him saying, *Suck it up sister. Trust Me. We have work to do.*

With all my might I come back with my best reminder to Him of how the waters all around me are raging.

The diagnosis my husband just received.

The stress of my workload.

Teenagers.

The overdraft fees piling up.

I'm exhausted and overwhelmed. I'm not sure I can take another step, much less a step in obedience.

"Accept My peace. Trust Me. Let Me lead you," I hear Him reply.

Read Joshua 3:7-16.

God promises Joshua that when the Israelites reach the Jordan River, the Ark of the Covenant (which represented the actual presence of God at the time) will lead them across the Jordan River.

The waters were raging when they reached the river's bank.

> It was the harvest season, and the Jordan was overflowing its banks. But as soon as the feet of the priests who were carrying the Ark touched the water at the river's edge, the water above that point began backing up a great distance away at a town called Adam, which

is near Zarethan. And the water below that point flowed on to the Dead Sea until the riverbed was dry. Then all the people crossed over near the town of Jericho. – Joshua 3:15-16 (NLT)

Whether your river of suffering and trials is overflowing or just slightly flooding around you, God offers us peace and guidance when we trust Him to make a dry path. His peace can replace our anxiety even in the most difficult of circumstances.

Let's do a quick inventory of the struggles, trials, difficulties, and/or suffering we are enduring today. What waters are raging around you today? (Jot down your answers here.)

_____

_____

_____

_____

_____

Read Psalm 25:1-10 (NIV) below, and choose one or two verses you can commit to memory this week. Underline or highlight these verses and return throughout the week to continue imprinting them on your heart.

1. In you, Lord my God, I put my trust.
2. I trust in you; do not let me be put to shame, nor let my enemies triumph over me.
3. No one who hopes in you will ever be put to shame but shame will come on those who are treacherous without cause.
4. Show me your ways, Lord, teach me your paths.
5. Guide me in your truth and teach me, for you are God my Savior, and my hope is in you all day long.
6. Remember, Lord, your great mercy and love, for they are from of old.

7. Do not remember the sins of my youth and my rebellious ways according to your love remember me, for you, Lord, are good.

8. Good and upright is the Lord; therefore he instructs sinners in his ways.

9. He guides the humble in what is right and teaches them his way.

10. All the ways of the Lord are loving and faithful toward those who keep the demands of his covenant.

Sister friend, I know your scars may be deep and your wounds may even be fresh. If you're hurting deeply and your waters are raging so high you can barely keep your head above water, breathe sister.

Let Psalm 25:1 melt on your heart.

Let Him guide you through the rough waters.

Ask those around you to pray you through the overflowing riverbanks.

Plant your face in the Word and hold on tight to the truth.

Trust Him.

Enough anxiety. More peace.

His peace can replace our anxiety even in the most difficult of circumstances.

ENOUGH SAID: AFTER READING TODAY'S lesson, let's capture a truth and take a step in obedience.

What did you hear God specifically say to you today through His Word?

_____

_____

_____

_____

How will you respond?

_____

_____

_____

_____

Project Rescue

But I trust in your unfailing love. I will rejoice because you have rescued me.

- Psalm 13:5 (NLT)

MY LIFE HAS BEEN JAM packed full of rescues. They come in all shapes and sizes. Some are epic and some just a blip on the radar.

Like the time I prayed for a new job, because new ownership had me crazy. The advertising agency I was working for was unexpectedly acquired, and let's just say the new management team didn't jive with me. While I thought the answer was another job, the rescue actually came in the form of another acquisition that was the perfect fit for me and my career. I didn't have to leave my current position, and I was still working with all my peeps. #CareerRescue

Or, the time I unexpectedly lost my sweet Aunt Jan. Because she was my first phone call in the morning and almost always the last one before I laid my head down at night, the grief hit me smack in the gut, and I didn't think I would crawl out of it. Ever.

My family had little hope for me as well. Then one day, the Holy Spirit and I had a serious come to Jesus convo about how donuts and cigarettes aren't the best remedy for dealing with a broken heart. (Yes, these were my go-to's. Sad, but true). God slowly but surely pulled me out of the grips of grief, and repeated to me what I'm sure He and Aunt Jan conjured up as the mantra for the breakthrough in my brokenness—*Pull it together, sister. You have work to do.*

And, then there's the small rescues like the time I was in mid-conversation with one of our beloved teenagers, and the desire to lose every marble left in my being rose up in me like a wave of fury I had never experienced.

Instead of wrecking yet another opportunity to show our children what adulthood actually looks like, I stood in that moment, red-faced, but calling on the One who can overshadow me with His Spirit. Lord, give me Your patience, Your gentleness and Your self-control. Jesus take the wheel before I drop-kick a teenager. And, He did.

My life could be defined quite simply as "Project Rescue." I wish I could say I've managed the anxiety that comes along with the rescues of life successfully, but who am I kidding? I'm hanging by a thread some days.

Just this morning I had a good ugly cry over my bank balance being in the red once again on a Monday. Lord, please help those bills not to clear until Friday. Why can't I add and subtract? #MathIsHard

The big and small rescues of life are hard to come by without trust in the Rescuer.

I love these verses in Exodus right before God parted the Red Sea, when Moses is encouraging the Israelites.

> "Just stand still and watch the Lord rescue you today. The Egyptians you see today will never be seen again. The Lord himself will fight for you. Just stay calm." – Exodus 14:13-14 (NLT)

Over the years, I've had my fair share of screw-ups, bad decisions, stressful times, and difficult seasons. As I look back, I see how God fights for me and rescues me time after time.

How He put a youth pastor in my life as a teenager that taught me how to pray and love people.

How He protected me from bad decision after bad decision in my twenties that could have caused disaster after disaster if I was in control.

How He made a way for me to have a career where I could be fulfilled, but also build the skills I would need to serve Him with the gifts He provided.

How He sent me the husband who fit me like no other after I prayed for nine years to love someone again.

How He created the miracle of all miracles for my family with the birth of my daughter.

How He brought me out of the deepest grief I could imagine after the unexpected death of a loved one.

Time after time, He has . . .

Gone before me.

Been right there with me.

Never failed me.

Given me wisdom that was not my own.

Sustained me.

Loved me in spite of me.

Let's do a quick inventory of times in your life when you know God has rescued you, fought for you, gone before you. Jot down those rescues here.

_____

_____

_____

_____

_____

I am so thankful for the rescues. But more than that, I'm grateful for the Rescuer.

> But now, O Jacob, listen to the Lord who created you. O Israel, the one who formed you says, "Do not be afraid, for I have ransomed you. I have called you by name; you are mine. When you go through deep waters, I will be with you. When you go through rivers of difficulty, you will not drown. When you walk through the fire of oppression, you will not be burned up; the flames will not consume you. For I am the Lord, your God, the Holy One of Israel, your Savior. – Isaiah 43:1-3 (NLT)

The Rescuer brings peace. His Word promises peace for us time after time. Read the following verses and make a note of the promise of peace for each one.

Verse: Promise/Message Regarding Peace:

Acts 10:36

_____

Romans 15:13

_____

1 Corinthians 14:33

_____

2 Peter 1:2

_____

Anxiety, worry, stress doesn't make our load lighter. Trusting in the Rescuer does.

The irony that I'm writing this lesson on this day is pretty comical. Honestly, I'm in a season of anxiety. Maybe you are too. My mind can barely contemplate or even comprehend all the moving parts of life at the moment.

So, maybe it's time to call on the Rescuer?

My prayer, my shout out to the Rescuer, will be different from yours, but document your prayer of rescue here in the space below.

_____

_____

_____

_____

_____

My prayer today:

Father, I need You. I'm suffocating in anxiety, fear, worry, and the stress of life. So, today, I'm calling on You, my Rescuer. Fill my heart with Your peace. Consume my mind with Your hope and joy. Help me to discern the priorities of life that You have for me that would honor You, and to eliminate those that are simply emptiness I'm chasing. Give me Your perspective on every individual piece of worry and anxiety I'm harboring today. Rescue me from the stress, and show me practical steps to handle the load I'm carrying. Allow me to see these life circumstances how You see them. Change my perspective. Heal my heart from anxiety. Give me Your peace. In Jesus' name, Amen.

Let's say enough to the anxiety and call on our Rescuer today. Let's stand still and watch the Lord rescue us.

Enough anxiety. More peace.

Anxiety, worry, stress doesn't make our load lighter. Trusting in the Rescuer does.

ENOUGH SAID: AFTER READING TODAY'S lesson, let's capture a truth and take a step in obedience.

What did you hear God specifically say to you today through His Word?

_____

_____

_____

How will you respond?

_____

_____

_____

What Rules Your Heart?

And let the peace that comes from Christ rule in your hearts. For as members of one body you are called to live in peace. And always be thankful.

– Colossians 3:15 (NLT)

IN 2005, I WAS TWENTY-NINE and single. I had been in the advertising business for about eight years at that point, and because I grew up the daughter of a land-developer, I had the grand idea of starting a magazine for home builders in my home state. Advertising meets construction—how could this go wrong?

So, I quit my job and started my own magazine.

I launched *Building Arkansas Magazine* in May of 2005, without one ounce of prayer over it. Initially, the magazine took off—the feedback from home builders was great and the roster of advertisers was growing month-over-month. By early 2008, I had a small staff and I was finally in the black most months, cash flowing into my very own publishing company.

I was living the dream. My hope for what I just knew my career should be had become a reality, and I put everything I had into the business.

Then, just like that, the bottom fell out.

The recession of 2008 hit and took its toll on the building industry not only in Arkansas, but nationwide. Advertisers began pulling out of their existing contracts. Home builders went out of business. The industry was in shambles. *Building Arkansas Magazine* did not survive.

The square footage of my heart was consumed with my career, my success, and my status as a business owner. I had no room in my heart for all things Jesus: His will, His work, His truth.

I put my hope in everything but Jesus, and then I was surprised that my heart was riddled by anxiety.

The square-footage of our heart has a price per foot. What consumes us, rules us. So, as we wrap up this week, let's examine how much square footage anxiety is taking up in our heart of hearts.

What is your hope in today?

Check off which of the following apply to you.

O I put my hope in my career.

O I put my hope in my marriage.

O I put my hope in pleasing my parents.

O I put my hope in friendships.

O I put my hope in my kids and their achievements.

O I put my hope in how much money I earn.

O I put my hope in _____

(fill in the blank)

Family, career, achievements are all excellent aspirations for us all, but when we put our hope in anything but Jesus, we will be disappointed. Every time. This type of disappointment leads to anxiety, stress, worry, the need for control, unneeded pressure, and a host of other ailments that wreak havoc on our souls.

In John chapter eight, Jesus is having a fiery debate with the Pharisees and the people who had gathered on that particular day. They are arguing about who Jesus really is, and you can almost hear the frustration in Jesus' voice through His dialogue.

Read John 8:31-59.

In the first part of this passage, Jesus is declaring that truth sets us free; however, the people took Him very literal, proclaiming they had never been slaves, as they were descendants of Abraham, and in verse thirty-seven, He says . . .

"Yes, I realize that you are descendants of Abraham. And yet some of you are trying to kill me because there's no room in your hearts for my message." – John 8:37 (NLT)

And in verse forty-two and forty-three, He continues to plead His case that He is who He says He is, and God the Father sent Him.

Jesus told them, "If God were your Father, you would love me, because I have come to you from God. I am not here on my own, but he sent me. Why can't you understand what I am saying? It's because you can't even hear me!" – John 8:42-43 (NLT)

While we're not debating the identity of Jesus as the Messiah like the people were in this passage, we do struggle with the same issues the Pharisees and people of that day did: the square footage of our hearts and our ability to hear the voice of God in our lives. It's a double-edged conundrum of sorts. And, it begs two questions:

What is occupying square footage in our hearts?

Can we hear the voice of God in our lives?

Think about these two questions, and jot down your answers in the space below.

_____

_____

_____

_____

When anything but Jesus takes up square footage in our heart, it makes it tremendously difficult to fight off anxiety. But, when we fill our heart with God's Word, His promises, hope in Him alone, we make room for more peace and less anxiety. Our hearts begin to light up in our identity in Christ, and the result is a confident hope in who we are, our future, and the peace that comes with all that goodness.

I pray that your hearts will be flooded with light so that you can understand the confident hope he has given to those he called—his holy people who are his rich and glorious inheritance. – Ephesians 1:18 (NLT)

Anxiety has held us captive long enough. As we wrap up this week, let's recap how we can confront anxiety in our lives.

Let's replace worry with trust in Him.

Let's replace control with His agenda.

Let's replace the pain from trials and struggles with His purpose.

Let's replace the stress of life with hope in the rescue.

The reality of anxiety is inevitable. How we handle it directly affects our ability to effectively get on mission. Because, how can a girl really get busy for Jesus when anxiety, stress, and worry are dominating the headlines in her heart and mind? It's impossible. That's why it's time to say enough.

When anything but Jesus takes up square footage in our heart, it makes it tremendously difficult to fight off anxiety.

ENOUGH SAID: AFTER READING TODAY'S lesson, let's capture a truth and take a step in obedience.

What did you hear God specifically say to you today through His Word?

_____

_____

_____

_____

How will you respond?

_____

_____

_____

_____

Let's say enough to the anxiety that's ruling our lives.

It's long overdue.

Enough anxiety. More peace.

Enough of me. More of Jesus.

Week 4:

Enough *distractions*. More MISSION.

So you see, we are shown to be right with God by what we do, not by faith alone.

– James 2:24 (NLT)

IT WAS A SATURDAY NIGHT, and we were hanging out with two other dear couple friends of ours. It was a gripe-fest really. Who can one-up the other on how broke we are, how the kids have us on the verge of pulling our hair out, and how our careers are depleting every last ounce of energy we have. It was a pathetic meeting of the minds on how exhausted we all were with life. #FirstWorldProblems

And, then out of the blue, one of the guys said he had the remedy for our weariness. "Road trip!" he said.

"Ummmmm . . . did you hear the part about how broke we all are mister?" the sensible (female) adults in the discussion exclaimed.

Our dear friend had a Groupon for a condo rental in Florida, and he convinced all of us it was a great idea to head down to Florida for four days and take a break from life. We would leave on Thursday, crash in a condo in Destin, Florida, where he was sure we could all six sleep comfortably, and return back to Arkansas on Sunday.

It didn't take us long to say, "We're in!" and two days later, the girls hopped in my girlfriend's minivan and the guys took off in our old, white Chevy Tahoe.

I had the time of my life laughing and chatting it up with my girlfriends all the way to the Redneck Riviera. We pretty much solved all the world's problems, and laughed so hard we nearly. . . well, you know.

Our last stop before the condo was at a gas station just outside of Mobile, Alabama. If you've ever gone down to Florida via Mobile, you know once you're there, you can literally smell the beach. We were so excited!

"Next stop, toes in the sand!" I hollered at the fellas as they were jumping in the white Tahoe we had been following the entire day. And we took off.

About 20 minutes later, as I was driving my friend's mini-van, I felt like we were not going the right way, but I was following my husband, so I didn't think much of it. *Surely, he had his GPS on like he had the entire day.*

Almost an hour later, I knew we weren't going the right way. I had been down to Destin before, and this wasn't looking familiar. We were in the boondocks of Florida, and I'm pretty sure if we had stopped and gotten out of the vehicle we would have been attacked by alligators in these parts.

So, I interrupted my convo with the gals, and dialed up the hubs to check on our ETA for the condo.

Me: *Hey babe, are you sure this is the right way, I feel like we're in the boondocks and nowhere near the beach.*

Hubs: *Ummm . . . we're almost there honey, can't you see the beach?*

Me: *Nope.*

Hubs: *Where are you?*

I can't provide you with the remainder of that conversation, because I had what my husband likes to call a "Kate Plus Eight" moment once I realized I was indeed following a different white Tahoe than my own.

Long story short: remember how earlier in this study I told you I needed no-line bifocals because I don't see very well now that I'm forty and every last ounce of me is falling apart? Yep. That Tahoe I had been following for over an hour wasn't mine. We were lost and about to be gator bait.

Bottom line: I was distracted and found myself completely off course.

Sometimes my walk with Christ is much the same. I have great goals, objectives, steps to take, and mission to complete. The Holy Spirit has handed down my very own God assignments, opened doors of opportunity, and planted seeds of obedience and mission in my heart and mind. But sometimes these seeds aren't sown because I get off track.

I'm distracted in my Jesus journey, and my gut tells me maybe you are too.

Our days are full of interference. We find ourselves wedged between the mission God has for us and the intrusions of this crazy life.

This week is a call-to-action. I pray it's an elbow in your side to kick-start your mission. A bold nudge for you to bear your very own fruit.

> "I am the true grapevine, and my Father is the gardener. He cuts off every branch of mine that doesn't produce fruit, and he prunes the branches that do bear fruit so they will produce even more. You have already been pruned and purified by the message I have given you. Remain in me, and I will remain in you. For a branch cannot produce fruit if it is severed from the vine, and you cannot be fruitful unless you remain in me.
>
> Yes, I am the vine; you are the branches. Those who remain in me, and I in them, will produce much fruit. For apart from me you can do nothing." – John 15:1-5 (NLT)

Jesus is the grapevine.

God is the gardener.

Your mission is the fruit—the possibilities of what your life can produce for His Kingdom and His glory.

We were all uniquely and wonderfully made with a distinctive mission and specific fruit to bear. My mission isn't the same as yours. My fruit basket doesn't look like yours. But we all have a mission, and I'm confident we all have distractions that derail our mission from time to time.

This week, we're going to plot our way through the interruptions that stand in the way of our mission, and hopefully develop an action plan against these distractions.

We find ourselves wedged between the mission God has for us and the intrusions of this crazy life.

We are called to navigate people to Jesus—to be on mission.

We were made to glorify God in our everyday lives—to live out true mission.

It's time to say enough to the distractions in life so we can bear much fruit.

Enough interruptions.

Enough interference.

Enough distractions. More mission.

That Time Mary & Joseph Lost Jesus

I brought glory to you here on earth by completing the work you gave me to do.

— John 17:4 (NLT)

CONFESSIONS OF A PARENT OF teenagers: I will stalk a mobile phone like a hawk. If you're a teen in my household, I will know where you are, who you're with, and can literally drop a pin on your location at any given moment. So, when you're driving around cruisin' Sonic don't think Momma doesn't know. I'm on you like the FBI on a known terrorist. Can I get a hands-raised emoji for the stalker apps that help track our teens?

We have two teenage boys in our household, and they couldn't be any different. At this juncture in their lives, one has a car (the seventeen-year-old) and one does not (fifteen going on thirty-five). Ironically enough, my teenager-tracking ninja skills require more savviness with the younger pup than when tracking the one who actually owns a vehicle. The senior in high school is quite predictable in his travels—school, work, church, home—these are the four main destinations in his weekly schedule. The younger lad on the other hand, I'm not gonna lie, I track him most days simply through his Snapchat story.

He snapped his lunch in the cafeteria—hallelujah he made it to school!

Snapped an unofficial wrestling match among his buddies in the church parking lot, shenanigans before Jesus. I'll take it.

A snap of his friend's new dog with the funny name—confirmed location at said friend's house.

His pin drops several times a day, but you better believe he will never be accused of not making the most of his teenage years. It's gonna be a fun ride y'all. Please fill my inbox with advice for parenting a rowdy teenager ASAP!

I'm sure Mary and Joseph wished for *Find My Friends* on a mobile device 2,000 years ago. You remember? That time they lost Jesus for a hot minute.

> Every year Jesus' parents went to Jerusalem for the Passover festival. When Jesus was twelve years old, they attended the festival as usual. After the celebration was over, they started home to Nazareth, but Jesus stayed behind in Jerusalem. His parents didn't miss him at first, because they assumed he was among the other travelers. But when he didn't show up that evening, they started looking for him among their relatives and friends.
>
> When they couldn't find him, they went back to Jerusalem to search for him there. Three days later they finally discovered him in the Temple, sitting among the religious teachers, listening to them and asking questions. All who heard him were amazed at his understanding and his answers.
>
> His parents didn't know what to think. "Son," his mother said to him, "why have you done this to us? Your father and I have been frantic, searching for you everywhere."
>
> "But why did you need to search?" he asked. "Didn't you know that I must be in my Father's house?" But they didn't understand what he meant.
>
> Then he returned to Nazareth with them and was obedient to them. And his mother stored all these things in her heart.
> – Luke 2:41-51 (NLT)

Three days. Mary and Joseph were panicked for three whole days searching for the Son of God. Can you imagine?

We've lost Jesus. The Messiah is gone. This is going to be a big problem, they must have thought.

Mary and Joseph were distracted. The Bible doesn't tell us by what, how, or why, but clearly, they had taken their eyes off Jesus.

So, as we dig into this week's study of distractions, let's examine our hearts and minds for what is causing us to take our eyes off Jesus.

First, we'll ask ourselves some simple questions to get started.

Circle the answer to the questions below that you agree with most.

Are you distracted in your walk with Christ?   yes   no

Are there times when you take your eyes off Jesus?   yes   no

Now, let's dig a little deeper.

What category do your distractions fall into the most? (Circle the top 3 categories your distractions fall under most. Or, add your own categories if these don't fit your distractions.)

Family   Volunteering   Relationships

Career   Entertainment   Slumber

Now, let's take a look at those three categories you selected, and identify the specific distraction in the chart on the next page. Circle those that apply to you in the three categories you identified as having the most distractions in your walk with Christ. Fill in the blanks with additional distractions in your categories if applicable.

Disclaimer: I acknowledge these are not all negative distractions. Matter of fact, many of these are fantastic in every way. Some of these may apply to you and they're *not* distractions. For example, you can certainly serve in your local church *and* find a way to also participate and attend the services each week to be sure you're poured into regularly. Circle and/or fill in *only* the ones you feel are distractions. Let's allow the Holy Spirit to lead our pen to circle our answers on this one.

Circle and/or fill in your own distraction in the empty spaces under each category.

FAMILY	VOLUNTEERING	RELATIONSHIPS	CAREER	ENTERTAINMENT	SLUMBER
Issues with children	Community commitments that require a substantial time commitment	Spouse	I've established my identity in what I do for a living	Social media	Can a girl just lounge on the sofa (ALL the time)?
Aging parent	Committed to serving in my local church but not committed to attending services regularly	Friends	My work pulls me away from mission often	Recreational activities in the community (ball games, dance, etc.)	Naps mean more to me than mission
Health issue of family member(s)	Outside ministry projects that demand significant investment	Gossip group	At work, I'm not honoring and glorifying God	TV/Netflix/ Hulu & All Its Cousins	I just want to relax every day in every way

Now that you've circled and identified some of the main distractions, those circumstances and aspects of life that take your eyes off Jesus and His mission for you, let's complete one final task.

Review the distractions that you circled, and put a **star (*)** by the ones you *can* control and a **plus-sign (+)** next to the ones you *cannot* control.

+ Distractions I cannot control: Take a few minutes to pray over the distractions you *cannot* control (those with a plus-sign). Ask God to intervene in these circumstances. Ask Him to remove the circumstance as a distraction and show you how you can glorify Him right in the middle of it all.

* Distractions I can control: This is where the action plan comes in. For each distraction you *can* control (those with a star), let's write a brief action plan below to help remove the interruption and replace it with mission.

Distraction: **Action Plan to Replace with Mission:**

_____

_____

_____

_____

_____

Before I show up on your "I thought I liked her, but now I don't" list, please hear me again when I say these distractions don't have to be negative, or even be considered distractions; however, it's easy for our entertainment, our volunteering, our career, and even our families to distract us from Jesus and the mission we're called to in our lives.

I spend four weekends a year and more money than I want to admit on dance tuition, costumes, travel, and all things competitive dance for my seven-year-old. I'm a dance mom, and there are days it is a distraction to say the least. But there are also days when I pray with my daughter before she goes on stage and remind her everything she does should glorify God, even if it is by eight counts, under lights on a stage with eight of her besties. I spend hours at the dance studio on week nights chatting it up with the other moms, hopefully encouraging them, sharing this little light of mine, and navigating them to Jesus whenever possible.

It is a fine line we walk in these distractions, but if our gauge is focused on Jesus and if we're navigating others to Him and glorifying God while I'm adding rhinestones to fishnet tights and sharing way too many laughs with moms and daughters who might need to be reminded of the God who loves them, I am good with that. It's when I'm sacrificing my tithe for costumes or jumping on the gossip train in the dance studio lobby that it becomes a distraction.

Discernment is critical in our distractions. If circumstances, relationships, commitments seem like distractions, even for a season, it might be time to chat it up with the King of Kings and either remove or evaluate your focus.

We can be on mission in our everyday lives and our everyday moments. Fruit can produce anywhere when God is glorified, holiness reigns, and Jesus is the focus.

On the Sunday evening after Jesus had been crucified and then raised from the dead, He appeared to His disciples. Fill in the blanks below with Jesus' words before we wrap up today:

Again he said, "Peace be with you. As the Father has_____ me, so I am _____ you." – John 20:21 (NLT)

We have been called—sent out into our world for mission.

Let's say enough to the distractions we can control and commit to pray through the ones we can't.

Enough distractions. More mission.

Fruit can produce anywhere when God is glorified, holiness reigns and Jesus is the focus.

ENOUGH SAID: AFTER READING TODAY'S lesson, let's capture a truth and take a step in obedience.

What did you hear God specifically say to you today through His Word?

_____

_____

_____

_____

How will you respond?

_____

_____

_____

_____

Pull Yourself Together

Then Jesus said to his disciples, "Whoever wants to be my disciple must deny
themselves and take up their cross and follow me."

– Matthew 16:24 (NIV)

I HAVE THIS GROUP OF forever friends. We have this chant—it's a mantra really—our very own personal hymn of friendship. Those three merciful, encouraging, and in-your-face words we all need to hear at one point or another.

Pull yourself together.

Like, really—dig deep, and pull it together, sis.

I've been on the giving and receiving end of these words, and neither side is necessarily comfortable, but at times, they can be essential.

I can't count the times the Holy Spirit has terrorized me with these words, which is one of the reasons I recently delivered them to my friend who lost her job. Not just any job, but the job she had held for over a decade with a very prestigious company, in a very prestigious industry, with I'm sure a very prestigious paycheck. She had a pity party for several weeks, and I played my part in donating tissue, encouraging her that God had a plan for her, and began building her new resume even though she hadn't showered in almost a week.

And when the pity party got a little too rowdy and went on a little too long, I delivered the words she knew would eventually come out of my mouth: *pull yourself together.*

I know many of you are already writing me a scathing email about gentleness and encouragement for others, but hopefully you understand these are not words I would deal out to just any acquaintance. Honestly, these same words

118

have been distributed to me from the one who was hearing them from me on this particular day. We have been friends for almost two decades. We are sisters. I've changed her baby's diaper, held back her hair while she threw up, cried over ex-boyfriends, and basically grew up together. She expects nothing less from me, I assure you.

And, while you and I have only been hanging out for a few weeks now, I feel like we are tight, and hopefully you "get" me by now—all of my crazy, squirrel-chasing, hashtag lovin' self. Surely, it won't surprise you much when I dish out these three words on our journey together of saying enough to our distractions today.

With all the love in my heart, from all of me to all of you: *pull yourself together*.

If we're honest, I believe most of us have times in our lives when we need to pull it together. The mantra is simple, but taking the first step is tough.

Check out this story from Jesus' day. He had something to say to a sick man who had been lying on his mat just steps from healing for a very long time.

> Afterward Jesus returned to Jerusalem for one of the Jewish holy days. Inside the city, near the Sheep Gate, was the pool of Bethesda, with five covered porches. Crowds of sick people—blind, lame, or paralyzed—lay on the porches. One of the men lying there had been sick for thirty-eight years. When Jesus saw him and knew he had been ill for a long time, he asked him, "Would you like to get well?"
>
> "I can't, sir," the sick man said, "for I have no one to put me into the pool when the water bubbles up. Someone else always gets there ahead of me."
>
> Jesus told him, "Stand up, pick up your mat, and walk!"
>
> Instantly, the man was healed! He rolled up his sleeping mat and began walking! – John 5:1-9a (NLT)

In these verses, a sick man has a brief encounter with Jesus that changes everything. Jesus commands him to "Stand up, pick up your mat, and walk." So, he does. And, he's healed.

Some days I'm on my bed mat like this lame man. I'm comfortable and cozy there. And then, if I listen clearly, the Holy Spirit pushes me to pick up my mat and walk.

What if our comfort in *not* getting on missions *is* the distraction?

The porch of complacency is where mission is paralyzed. Sometimes our current state of comfort and contentment is the distraction standing between where we are today and where God can use us in a mighty way.

We like sitting on the sidelines, hanging out in our pew on Sundays, and opening our weekly devotional that pops up in our inbox every Saturday like clock-work. It's cozy and easy and predictable. But, is that really mission? Does that really result in the fruit that God's Word clearly describes?

Ask yourself the following questions and identify if it might be time to pick up your mat and take a few steps.

Has God been speaking to you about taking a specific action or step in faith, obedience or surrender that you have been ignoring? If so, list that step here.

_____

_____

_____

_____

Is there a sin or habit in your life God has asked you to remove, but you're holding on to it tightly knowing it would require a commitment you're just not ready for at this point?

_____

_____

_____

_____

Do you feel called to serve in some capacity in your local church, a local ministry, or global ministry, but you have not acted on that appeal from the Holy Spirit?

_____

_____

_____

_____

We have to do something different to be healed in a different way. We have to change our minds and our behavior to break out of our comfort zone.

I've gone through seasons where a number of things are preventing me from getting off my mat and walking in the purpose and plan God has for me: pride, jealousy, fear, lack of self-control, a bazillion excuses, my people pleasing agenda, and just plain ol' laziness. And, then the Holy Spirit whispers, "Pull it together, sis, we've got work to do."

So, I ever so slowly get off my mat, and take a step.

If you're in a season where you've gotten comfortable right where you are, **what is preventing you from picking up your mat and getting off the porch?** Taking these steps of obedience, ending these habits, or walking in to your calling? (Jot down your thoughts below and refer to your answers to the questions above.)

_____

_____

_____

_____

We are called to holiness and mission for the One who gave it all.

God has called us to live holy lives, not impure lives. Therefore, anyone who refuses to live by these rules is not disobeying

human teaching but is rejecting God, who gives his Holy Spirit
to you. – 1 Thessalonians 4:7-8 (NLT)

If you've been on the porch of complacency for far too long, it's time to
say enough. We can't get comfortable where mission doesn't live. So, will you
join me in bidding farewell to that mat you're hanging out on today?

Enough distractions. More mission.

We can't get comfortable where mission doesn't live.

ENOUGH SAID: AFTER READING TODAY'S lesson, let's capture a truth and
take a step in obedience.

What did you hear God specifically say to you today through His Word?

_____

_____

_____

_____

How will you respond?

_____

_____

_____

_____

The Voices in My Head

Walk with the wise and become wise; associate with fools and get in trouble.

– Proverbs 13:20 (NLT)

AS I'M WRITING TODAY, IT'S Crazytown up in here at Camp Peters. Our seven-year-old has strep throat, so my husband is taking care of her, and I use the term "taking care of" very loosely. She's currently singing every country song my husband has on iTunes at the top of her lungs. The perfect remedy for strep, right? I'm pretty sure it's inappropriate on every level for my seven-year-old daughter to bolt out *Body Like a Back Road* like she truly means every word. Don't judge. I'm 99% sure she has no clue.

My neighbor has decided this is the perfect weekend to mow, blow, and trim his entire oasis of lawn perfection. And, our teenagers are begging to jump on Netflix in the room adjacent to where I write, but I can't focus with an episode of *Grey's Anatomy* blaring. Yes, of all the things they could watch, they're binging on McDreamy's every word. I'm doing my best y'all! #PickYourBattles

Needless to say, distractions are at an all-time high for me today—primarily interruptions of the noisy kind from every single voice inside Camp Peters.

The voices around us are powerful influences in our lives. They can lead us into or away from mission in a flash. We have both inside and outside voices—external influencers who chime in often, and internal voices inside our heart and mind that can lead us down the right path or distract us in every way.

I've been in women's ministry for years now, and I can tell you that hearing the voice of God clearly is a challenge I hear about often. I'm confident we believe He speaks to us, but I'm also convinced it can be difficult discerning His voice.

One night Eli, who was almost blind by now, had gone to bed. The lamp of God had not yet gone out, and Samuel was sleeping in the Tabernacle near the Ark of God. Suddenly the Lord called out, "Samuel!"

"Yes?" Samuel replied. "What is it?" He got up and ran to Eli. "Here I am. Did you call me?"

"I didn't call you," Eli replied. "Go back to bed." So he did.

Then the Lord called out again, "Samuel!"

Again Samuel got up and went to Eli. "Here I am. Did you call me?"

"I didn't call you, my son," Eli said. "Go back to bed."

Samuel did not yet know the Lord because he had never had a message from the Lord before. So the Lord called a third time, and once more Samuel got up and went to Eli. "Here I am. Did you call me?"

Then Eli realized it was the Lord who was calling the boy. So he said to Samuel, "Go and lie down again, and if someone calls again, say, 'Speak, Lord, your servant is listening.'" So Samuel went back to bed.

And the Lord came and called as before, "Samuel! Samuel!"

And Samuel replied, "Speak, your servant is listening." – 1 Samuel 3:2-10 (NLT)

Discerning the voice of God is critical to our mission. When we're distracted by all of the noise around us, we can't hear what God has to say.

Let's dissect some ways we can hear the voice of God louder in our lives, and identify how we can remove the distractions of other voices that shouldn't be so loud.

For those of us who have a relationship with Jesus, we have the privilege of the Holy Spirit residing in our hearts. He is a cheerleader for mission in our lives.

"But I will send you the Advocate—the Spirit of truth. He will come to you from the Father and will testify all about me." – John 15:26 (NLT)

The voice of the Holy Spirit begs to be the loudest in our life, but our hearts and minds are crowded with other voices fighting for the mic.

We have three main voices in our heart and mind: our own voice, the enemy's voice, and the voice of the Holy Spirit.

I don't know about you, but when my voice and the enemy's voice get together, it's a recipe for disaster. But, when the Holy Spirit is the loudest voice in my life, I'm much more inclined to pursue mission and produce fruit.

Let's do a quick analysis to identify where we are in our communication with the Holy Spirit today. First, below write ways you believe the Holy Spirit speaks to you. What are His avenues of communication to you personally?

_____

_____

_____

_____

Next, write a statement that defines your communication with the Holy Spirit today. Above you wrote *how* He communicates with you, here include a description of the current state of that communication: is it frequent, rich, lacking, intimate, personal, etc.

_____

_____

_____

_____

Because discernment is so critical, I think we have to do a "gut check" when we're questioning is this God's voice, my own voice, or even worse, the voice of the enemy.

Let's do a quick analysis of the characteristics of the Holy Spirit's voice compared to our own or the enemy's. Review the comparison on the next page and add your thoughts on additional characteristics of each.

Holy Spirit's Voice	My Voice	The Enemy's Voice
Directs me to Jesus Leads to peace	Distracts me from my mission Supports a selfish balance	Encourages to stay in my mess Creates chaos

The common denominators in my life that exist when I'm hearing the voice of God clearly include:

When I'm spending consistent time in the Word

When I'm recognizing my sin, repenting, and making efforts to change

When I'm journaling in my quiet time and documenting what God is saying to me through His Word and my personal prayers to Him

What about you? What do the habits and circumstances in your life look like when you're hearing God loud and clear? List those below.

_____

_____

_____

_____

Side note: If you've recently come into a relationship with Jesus, and you're panicking because you have never "heard" from God, I want to be clear that

I don't audibly hear the Lord speak to me. Sometimes it's as powerful as the loudest voice I've ever heard, but it is in my spirit. I'm sure if I asked every reader of this study how they hear the voice of God in their lives I would get a multitude of answers. That's how amazing our God is! He speaks to us in our unique way, but we have to position ourselves to hear Him.

There are times in my life when I have been able to hear the Holy Spirit loud and clear, but there have definitely been seasons when I wondered if God was even there.

As we wrap up today, let's fill in the blanks below as a reminder that God is always there:

So do not fear, for I am with you; do not be dismayed, for I am your God.

I will _____ you and _____ you; I will uphold you with my righteous right hand. – Isaiah 41:10 (NIV)

The distractions that stand between where we are today and where God wants to use us include the voices in our lives. We must position ourselves to hear the voice of God so we can respond to His calling and get on mission.

Enough distractions. More mission.

He speaks to us in our unique way, but we have to position ourselves to hear Him.

ENOUGH SAID: AFTER READING TODAY'S lesson, let's capture a truth and take a step in obedience.

What did you hear God specifically say to you today through His Word?

_____

_____

_____

_____

How will you respond?

_____

_____

_____

_____

Is God Waiting on Me?

So, my dear brothers and sisters, be strong and immovable. Always work enthusiastically for the Lord, for you know that nothing you do for the Lord is ever useless.

– 1 Corinthians 15:58 (NLT)

FOR ALMOST TEN YEARS THE Holy Spirit harassed me—pushed me to DO SOMETHING. I had spent almost twenty years (it hurts to even type that) climbing the corporate ladder. It was fun, and challenging, and has taught me more than I could have ever imagined. But, I was still empty. Unfulfilled. Full of great accomplishment in my career (because I do LOVE what I do!), but knowing I was made for more.

So, I began to pray for a breakthrough. I felt this tug on my heart to serve God in a bigger way, but wasn't sure what that looked like. And then I got a text from my pastor's wife.

Stacey: *Hey girl! You wanna grab lunch tomorrow?*

(Long pause—I had never been invited to lunch by the pastor's wife. *What was this about?*)

Me: *Sure! Name the time and place.*

Stacey: *Two Sisters Café—11:30. See ya then!*

At the time, Stacey and I were not "going to lunch" kind of friends. We were certainly friends, but in a "Hey girl, how are you?" kind of way. So, I began to frantically search my Facebook timeline.

Had I posted something completely inappropriate that called for a lunch meeting with the first lady? That was a real possibility.

After a quick review of my social feeds full of ridiculous pictures of my daughter and rants about the current state of the Arkansas Razorbacks football team, I concluded my social media posts were not the reason for this meeting.

My husband and our pastor are dear friends, so I thought maybe Stacey wanted to chat it up about the boys? Or, maybe she wanted to pick my brain about advertising and marketing? After all, at the time she was the campus director for the central campus of That.Church. (Yes, I attend a church called That.Church. How fun is that?).

Maybe the church needed some marketing assistance and she thought I could help?

I was wrong on all levels.

So, after being on pins and needles for twenty-four hours, I sat across the table at Two Sisters Café in Sherwood, Arkansas, waiting to hear what Stacey had on her mind. Notebook and Bible in hand, she sat down with a big smile.

She had one question. "Would you be interested in serving as my assistant leader in a new women's ministry I'm launching at the church?"

My first thought was . . . *Um, no. I can't lead in ministry, I'm a mess!*

But that voice of the Holy Spirit that we talked about yesterday closed my lips, and I mustered up a quick response. I replied with a simple, "I'll pray about that," as I enjoyed the best grilled chicken strawberry salad I had ever put in my mouth.

A week or so later, after wrestling with the Holy Spirit (He won!), I sent Stacey the "I'm in!" text I hope she was praying for.

What I didn't fully realize at the time is that Stacey was completely revamping our women's ministry in response to nudge after nudge of the Holy Spirit leading her. Little did she know, it wouldn't be long before God had hundreds of women on Wednesday nights sitting in the worship center of That.Church, in homes around the country watching online, and at various satellite campuses attending a ministry called Real Women. The vision God put on her heart became a reality and then some.

That lunch date turned into the declaration of mission in this season of my life, and I am so grateful to play my part. Not only has Stacey become one of my dearest friends in every possible way, but we are still on this journey together, and God continues to amaze us every day.

What I know for sure is that before that lunch date, I was distracted waiting on Him, when in reality, He was waiting on me. I had been sitting back waiting on God to declare that I was worthy of His mission, but I didn't believe it until Stacey's one question breathed life into the tug I had felt in my heart.

Today, we're going to dissect this idea of the distraction in waiting. Are we distracted waiting on Him, when in reality He is waiting on us?

Read John 11:1-37, and let's look at these verses for some wisdom.

Quick recap: the brother of Mary and Martha, Lazarus, had become very ill. Jesus was in another area at the time, so the two sisters sent word to Jesus that Lazarus was very sick in hopes that He would come heal him. Jesus acknowledged that Lazarus's sickness would not end in death, but in God's glory (John 11:4). However, Lazarus died and Mary, Martha, and her family were weeping and wailing over his death. Four days later, Jesus comes to them, and we're going to pick up the Scripture when they end up at the tomb where Lazarus had been placed.

> Jesus was still angry as he arrived at the tomb, a cave with a stone rolled across its entrance. "Roll the stone aside," Jesus told them.
>
> But Martha, the dead man's sister, protested, "Lord, he has been dead for four days. The smell will be terrible."
>
> Jesus responded, "Didn't I tell you that you would see God's glory if you believe?" So they rolled the stone aside. Then Jesus looked up to heaven and said, "Father, thank you for hearing me. You always hear me, but I said it out loud for the sake of all these people standing here, so that they will believe you sent me." Then Jesus shouted, "Lazarus, come out!" And the dead man came out, his hands and feet bound in graveclothes, his face wrapped in a headcloth. Jesus told them, "Unwrap him and let him go!" – John 11:38-44 (NLT)

This story is a beautiful reminder that we can get distracted waiting on God to declare something in our lives, when in reality He already has.

What are you waiting for God to declare in your life? (Jot down your thoughts below.)

_____

_____

_____

_____

Is it possible you're waiting on God, when really He's waiting on you?

_____

_____

_____

Sometimes the first step away from our distractions and into mission is a simple one.

For me it was saying "I'm in!"

For you it might be praying for an opportunity to serve, taking a simple step in obedience, walking out of your comfort zone, or grabbing a friend and inviting her to read this Bible study with you.

What is one simple step you can take to get on mission today?

_____

_____

Sister, I know it can be scary, uncomfortable, and even weird to take these steps of obedience in mission. But these first steps produce the bud of the fruit in mission. These steps breathe life into the calling God has for you. I urge you (I beg you!). Make that phone call. Sign up for that ministry. Invite that friend to small group. Start that Bible study at work. Pray with that hurting friend.

Take a step. Do something.

If today, as you're analyzing this notion of the distraction of waiting on God to declare something before you take that first step, I want to remind you that His work through you doesn't depend on you. He will equip you. He will use you in spite of you. I am living proof.

And I am certain that God, who began the good work within you, will continue his work until it is finally finished on the day when Christ Jesus returns. – Philippians 1:6 (NLT)

The distraction of waiting is an easy one to overlook. I pray we say enough to the waiting today and declare mission in our lives.

Enough distractions. More mission.

We can get distracted waiting on God to declare something in our lives, when in reality He already has.

ENOUGH SAID: AFTER READING TODAY'S lesson, let's capture a truth and take a step in obedience.

What did you hear God specifically say to you today through His Word?

_____

_____

_____

_____

How will you respond?

_____

_____

_____

_____

Goodbye Distractions. Hello Mission!

We must quickly carry out the tasks assigned us by the one who sent us. The night is coming, and then no one can work.

– John 9:4 (NLT)

IN JUNE OF 2014, MY husband, Coby, had a heart attack and ended up having quintuple bypass surgery at the ripe old age of forty-four. Talk about a distraction.

I had been out of town traveling for work when I got the call. "Mrs. Peters, you need to come home immediately, your husband is having open heart surgery in the morning." So, I jumped on a plane, landed in Little Rock early the next morning, hitched a ride to the hospital, and when I walked in they were prepping him for surgery.

The surgery went well. Five days later they were rolling him out of the hospital entrance, and he slowly but surely got in the car to head home. It had been a long week for both of us, and we were ready to get back to our new normal that would include healthy eating, exercising, and taking better care of ourselves.

We pulled out of the Arkansas Heart Hospital, and there it was just two blocks down the road—the blinking red "Hot Now" sign at Krispy Kreme calling our names. It felt like a sick joke.

Half a dozen warm glazed donuts later, with icing on our lips and shame in our hearts, we pulled back onto the path of heading home, and we were sure we would never be the same. Not because of the two pounds we had just gained, but because we knew the weight of every decision we made moving forward could have significant impact on our future and the future of our family.

Sometimes distractions get the best of us. Even if they don't come with flashing red lights luring us in it's easy to get caught up in the emptiness of all that is holding us back.

So, today as we wrap up this week of jump-starting our mission, let's walk through a familiar story of Jesus and His disciples, and say goodbye to our distractions once and for all.

Read Matthew 14:22-33.

Now, let's look at this story and see what we can learn together. To set the stage, remember, Jesus had just fed over 5,000 people with five loaves of bread and two fish. Our story picks up immediately after that miraculous meal, and I believe there are six simple truths we can capture from this Scripture. Let's dig in.

1. God insists we embark on mission by way of His instruction.

Matthew 14:22 tells us Jesus insisted His disciples get back into the boat and cross to the other side of the lake while He sent the people home.

> Turn my eyes from worthless things, and give me life through your word. – Psalm 119:37 (NLT)

2. Time alone with Him is essential.

Matthew 14:23 says that after Jesus sent the people home, He went up into the hills to pray alone.

> Rejoice in our confident hope. Be patient in trouble, and keep on praying. – Romans 12:12 (NLT)

3. The circumstances won't always be ideal.

Matthew 14:24 tells us that the disciples were in trouble. A storm had come up and they were fighting heavy waves.

> "I have told you all this so that you may have peace in me. Here on earth you will have many trials and sorrows. But take heart, because I have overcome the world." – John 16:33 (NLT)

4. God is right here with us. Always.

Matthew 14:27 says that as Jesus walked on the water toward the disciples, He told them not to fear, because He was there.

> I will go before you and will level the mountains; I will break down gates of bronze and cut through bars of iron. – Isaiah 45:2 (NIV)

5. The rescue comes with a lesson.

Matthew 14:31 says after Peter took a few steps toward Jesus he began to sink. But Jesus immediately grabbed him, asking him *"Why did you doubt Me?"*

> Now may the God of peace—who brought up from the dead our Lord Jesus, the great Shepherd of the sheep, and ratified an eternal covenant with his blood—may he equip you with all you need for doing his will. May he produce in you, through the power of Jesus Christ, every good thing that is pleasing to him. All glory to him forever and ever! Amen. – Hebrews 13:20-21 (NLT)

6. God is who He says He is.

Matthew 14:32-33 tells us after they were rescued, the disciples exclaimed, *"You really are the Son of God!"*

> Jesus told him, "I am the way, the truth, and the life. No one can come to the Father except through me. – John 14:6 (NLT)

Which of these six truths do you connect with the most today and why? Write your thoughts below.

_____

_____

_____

_____

Which of these truths do you need to be reminded of most today?

_____

_____

_____

_____

As we wrap up this week, let's be on alert for the distractions that can paralyze our mission.

O Let's remember we have a mission to bear our own unique fruit.

O Let's remove the distractions we can control, and pray through the ones we can't.

O Let's position ourselves in a way that the Holy Spirit is the loudest voice in our life.

O Let's replace distractions with mission.

This week we developed an action plan to combat the interruptions that stand in the way of our mission. It's time to take the first step.

It's time to take the first step.

ENOUGH SAID: AFTER READING TODAY'S lesson, let's capture a truth and take a step in obedience.

What did you hear God specifically say to you today through His Word?

_____

_____

_____

_____

How will you respond?

_____

_____

_____

_____

Let's say enough to the distractions that are tripping us up.

Goodbye to empty interference.

Enough distractions. More mission.

Enough of me. More of Jesus.

Week 5:

Enough *leaving Him out.* More INVITING HIM IN.

Come close to God, and God will come close to you. Wash your hands, you sinners; purify your hearts, for your loyalty is divided between God and the world.

– James 4:8 (NLT)

MY DAUGHTER STELLA WAS FOUR weeks old. It was my first (and only) maternity leave, and all I knew was that I needed adult conversation in the worst possible way. The hubs had gone back to work after two weeks, and I had spent every waking moment with the new love of my life, but she wasn't much of a companion with her cycle of sleeping, eating, and pooping.

Thankfully, my mom rescued me with a simple text. *Let's have brunch tomorrow!*

I couldn't wait to leave the house, put on some make up, and rejoin the land of the living after four weeks at home with a newborn. The idea of brunch sounded like manna from Heaven.

I packed the baby in the car with every possible baby item I might need on my trip to brunch with Mom, and headed to one of our favorite spots in Little Rock. When I pulled into the parking lot of the restaurant, I scored a parking spot on the front row just steps from the door. Mom was waiting outside waving big with a smile on her face.

I jumped out of the car, grabbed my purse, clicked my keyless remote to lock the car, and started toward Mom with my arms wide open for a big hug.

Suddenly, Mom's smile turned to concern. "What about the baby?"

Oh yeah. I have a baby. #MomFail

Four-week-old Stella was the guest of honor at this particular brunch, and I almost left her out from the get-go.

It was only four short steps, but my heart sunk. Did I really just forget I was a mom? It was my first real feeling of mom-shame. And, dang did it sting!

Since then I've had more mom fails than I care to count. Grace wins, mommas! Can I get an Amen?

Hold on tight my friend, because this week we're wading through challenging waters. We're considering tough questions relating to where we've put God in our lives. Have we invited Him into our friendships, our lawn chair conversations at the ballpark, our fancy-pants planning, and every area of life? Or, are we hitting the button on the keyless remote, and walking away from the Guest of Honor?

It's time for a gut check. I believe if our hearts were exposed, we would be forced to admit that sometimes it's comfortable, or dare I say convenient, to leave God out of the routine of life. But, our relationship with the King of Kings was designed for more.

Jesus made it possible for Heaven and earth to collide in our lives every day. When we invite Him in to our thoughts, actions, conversations, and relationships, we experience Him in the whole shebang. His presence changes everything.

> You will show me the way of life, granting me the joy of your presence and the pleasures of living with you forever. – Psalm 16:11 (NLT)

Living life in step with the Creator is powerful.

Inviting Him in breeds joy. Shines light. Produces fruit. Unleashes love.

When He seeps into our every day, we become undone in the best possible way.

This week, God's Word will be our guide, and my hope is that we will say enough to leaving God out and reconnect our world with the Savior who longs to be a part of it all.

I don't know about you, but my daily routine could use a shake-up. So, let's dig in and let Him invade our lives.

When we stop and listen, our hearts open.

When we unwrap the Word, it's an intervention for our soul.

When He seeps into our every day, we become undone in the best possible way.

He is waiting to be invited into every nook and cranny of our lives.

Enough excluding the guest of honor.
Enough abandoning connection with Him.
Enough leaving Him out. More inviting Him in.

The Main Character

So let us come boldly to the throne of our gracious God. There we will receive his mercy, and we will find grace to help us when we need it most.

– Hebrews 4:16 (NLT)

I SERVE IN WOMEN'S MINISTRY with an amazing team of women who challenge me, make me laugh, pick me up when I face plant, and encourage me to pluck my brows regularly (like now—shape those suckers up, sis!).

This summer our leader (one of my BFFs) scheduled a retreat for our Lead Team. We decided to head down to Hot Springs for a weekend to pray over the upcoming year, plan some things, and let's be real, have way too much fun.

A couple of weeks before the retreat, this post showed up on our Lead Team Facebook page:

We're going to an escape room while we're in Hot Springs at the retreat. Can't wait! #TeamBuilding

My response included both excitement: *I love an adventure!*

And, anxiety: *I stink at puzzles.*

If you've never participated in an escape room, let me break it down real quick. Basically you show up with your group (typically 4-8ish people). You're given a scenario and a goal to achieve. This can be anything from solve the murder mystery to save the universe from an evil empire to unlock the dungeon door. These escape rooms run the gamut, but there is a theme. If you achieve the goal, you escape. If you don't, you're not forever locked in the room—you just don't get to hold the "We escaped!" sign and tell your social media universe you are one smart cookie.

So, the two weeks leading up to our retreat, I concocted scenarios in my head of what the escape room experience might look like for our group. In reality, I was giving myself a pep-talk, because I felt like I had to prove myself to the group. I had been serving with them for years, but I felt compelled to show them my value. I didn't want to be booted off the island for bringing zero to the table when it came to sifting through the clues of an escape room.

When we arrived, I'm not gonna lie, the room we had signed up for was a little creepy. It was set back in the roaring twenties, during the gangster era in Hot Springs. A woman named Lily Rose had died (fictitiously), and we were challenged to find her spirit in the room. I know this isn't churchy or Jesus-like in any way, shape, or form, but we took the challenge.

Before the timer started (we had an hour to complete our task of finding the spirit of Lily Rose), the gentleman who ran the room informed us he would be watching our progress (on camera—yep, creepy!), and that we could ask for three clues during the course of the hour. Then he shut the door behind us. #LetTheGamesBegin

When I say it was mayhem, y'all, it was mayhem! Imagine five type-A women in full out chaos rummaging through an escape room digging for any clue they could find. I can't speak for the other women, but I was flying through that room trying to find and solve a clue as if my life depended on it because I thought my status in the group *did* depend on it.

We weren't really working together or focused on any one thing in particular. It was pandemonium for the first thirty minutes. I was red-faced, running around like a lunatic, battling my way through the trenches of this escape room like a boss. Who am I kidding? I was sweating bullets and had nothing to show for it.

When we were forty minutes in, without warning or solicitation of a clue, the escape room's clue-giver stopped us in our tracks.

Knock . . . knock . . . knock.

Don't forget about the main character: Lily Rose. The goal is to find the spirit of Lily Rose, he said.

Yeah, yeah, yeah, I thought. *I'm cementing my place on this team right now thank you very much. I ain't got time for Lily Rose!*

So, we kind of pulled it together, in a less chaotic, still-not-on-task kind of way . . . ish. One of our team members had surrendered. She was just staring blankly into space sitting on a sofa from 1923 that I'm pretty sure wasn't meant for perching. The rest of us had started to put together a puzzle, but we were getting nowhere fast.

Ten minutes left.

Knock . . . knock . . . knock.

Don't forget about Lily Rose. The goal is to find Lily Rose.

Five minutes left. The clock was ticking, and we were still pursuing our individual goals, which for me meant trying to earn my place on this team by proving to these women I was valuable—someone they wanted to serve in ministry with (which has *nothing* to do with how you perform in an escape room by the way).

Needless to say we didn't find the spirit of Lily Rose. Matter of fact, all I left with was a great story, some battle scars, and frizzy hair from sweating so much you would have thought I just left Zumba class.

Since that attempt at escape (or lack thereof), the Holy Spirit is constantly harassing me with gentle reminders as I go through the motions of my everyday life.

Knock . . . knock . . . knock.

Don't forget about the main character.

Don't forget about Jesus.

The clock is ticking.

The goal . . . the prize . . . the escape is Jesus. He is the main character.

Isn't life like an escape room? Hour by hour, day by day, the clock is winding down on our time here, and sometimes the goals we've set for ourselves don't include the main character. We're trapped in broken identities and expectations, living under the pressure of the world's standards, and occasionally inviting God in as an afterthought at best.

Our relationship with Jesus makes nearness to God available to us. When our hope is in Him, we aren't the star of the show, He is.

So prepare your minds for action and exercise self-control. Put all your hope in the gracious salvation that will come to you when Jesus Christ is revealed to the world. So you must live as God's obedient children. Don't slip back into your old ways of living to satisfy your own desires. You didn't know any better then. But now you must be holy in everything you do, just as God who chose you is holy. For the Scriptures say, "You must be holy because I am holy." – 1 Peter 1:13-16 (NLT)

Peter challenges us in these verses. Let's dig in and accept the challenge today.

1. Prepare your minds for action.

What does this mean to you?

_____

_____

_____

_____

_____

How can you accept this challenge with one step in obedience today?

_____

_____

_____

_____

_____

2. Don't satisfy your own desires.

What does this mean to you?

_____

_____

_____

_____

_____

How can you accept this challenge with one step in obedience today?

_____

_____

_____

_____

_____

3. Be holy in everything you do.

What does this mean to you?

_____

_____

_____

_____

_____

How can you accept this challenge with one step in obedience today?

_____

_____

_____

_____

_____

When we grab on tight to Jesus, invite Him into our lives in *everything* we do, holiness is possible. But if we've made ourselves the main character, we're putting our hope in our flesh, and abundant living is off the table.

Christ alone. He is our holiness. Our sustainer. Our shelter. Nothing compares.

> This I declare about the Lord: He alone is my refuge, my place of safety; he is my God, and I trust him. – Psalm 91:2 (NLT)

Maybe it's time for us to declare an invitation to the Lord. Write a prayer below inviting God into a specific area of your life today where you have been making yourself the main character. Ask Him to show up. And trust Him.

_____

_____

_____

_____

When we extend God an invitation to invade our lives, we're making a way for true abundant living.

Enough leaving Him out. More inviting Him in.

When our hope is in Him, we aren't the star of the show. He is.

ENOUGH SAID: **AFTER READING TODAY'S** lesson, let's capture a truth and take a step in obedience.

What did you hear God specifically say to you today through His Word?

_____

_____

_____

_____

How will you respond?

_____

_____

_____

_____

Nobody Puts Baby in a Corner

Let your roots grow down into him, and let your lives be built on him. Then your faith will grow strong in the truth you were taught, and you will over- flow with thankfulness.

– Colossians 2:7 (NLT)

ONE OF MY ALL-TIME FAVORITE movies is *Dirty Dancing*. Millennials, it's not what you think. Dial this one up on Netflix. It is a gem! (Caution: it is PG-13 in every possible way, so safeguard your littles.)

As I'm writing this, the movie is celebrating its 30th anniversary. It was your typical good girl falls for bad boy picture show, but not only did this cinematic gift help me fall in love with Patrick Swayze as a teenager, it also made me want to fight for the underdog.

The star of the movie, other than Swayze, was Jennifer Grey who played Baby, a young woman who's spending the summer at a sleepy resort with her parents. The resort becomes much less boring when she meets the dance instructor, Johnny (played by Swayze). Baby is determined to help Johnny perform the last big dance of the summer after his partner goes down from some unfortunate circumstances.

She was the underdog and everyone underestimated Baby: her dad, her mom, her sister, the resort staff. No one believed that she could have im- pact—that she even mattered really. Except for Johnny. After spending hours with Baby teaching her the dance they would perform, he realized he had miscalculated her impact not only in his dance, but in his life.

And, when Johnny shows up in the last scene of the movie, and proclaims, "Nobody puts Baby in a corner," it became one of the most famous lines in cinematic history.

There are t-shirts, memes, and coffee mugs. I might have bought the VHS tape and learned the entire dance at the end of the movie so I could perform it with the resort dancers every time I watched it. #JuniorHighMemories

When we underestimate people, circumstances, accomplishments, failures, and events in our lives, these miscalculations can cause us to make assumptions.

Just ask Nathanael.

At the conclusion of the first chapter of John, Jesus was recruiting His disciples, and they were following Him right and left. They had found the Messiah (v. 41), and they wanted to "come and see" (v. 39).

> Philip went to look for Nathanael and told him, "We have found the very person Moses and the prophets wrote about! His name is Jesus, the son of Joseph from Nazareth."
>
> "Nazareth!" exclaimed Nathanael. "Can anything good come from Nazareth?"
>
> "Come and see for yourself," Philip replied.
>
> As they approached, Jesus said, "Now here is a genuine son of Israel—a man of complete integrity."
>
> "How do you know about me?" Nathanael asked.
>
> Jesus replied, "I could see you under the fig tree before Philip found you."
>
> Then Nathanael exclaimed, "Rabbi, you are the Son of God—the King of Israel!"
>
> Jesus asked him, "Do you believe this just because I told you I had seen you under the fig tree? You will see greater things than this." Then he said, "I tell you the truth, you will all see heaven open and the angels of God going up and down on the Son of Man, the one who is the stairway between heaven and earth." – John 1:45-51 (NLT)

Can't you hear the assumption Nathanael was making? *Nazareth?! No one significant would come from Nazareth.* And, in just two sentences, Jesus set him straight.

Nathanael questioned who Jesus was, but Jesus never questioned who Nathanael was.

Sometimes we underestimate the impact God can have in our lives. Not because of where He's from, but because we've never truly invited Him into our everyday moments.

It's difficult to see God's impact when we're keeping Him at arm's length drawing near to Him in our pews and rows on Sundays, but rarely inviting Him anywhere outside the church house.

Is it possible, we're underestimating the power and the privilege of inviting God in our lives?

Today, let's play the "what-if" game with the power of God and the privilege of His presence in our lives.

First, let's look at the PRIVILEGE of inviting God into our lives from the vantage point of our flesh and the vantage point of grace.

My flesh says:	Grace says:
I *have* to invite God in.	It is *joy* to invite God in.
I *should* invite God in.	I *get to* invite God in.
I *better* invite God in.	It is an *honor* to invite God in.

Circle the statements above that your soul agrees with the most today.

> You will show me the way of life, granting me the joy of your presence and the pleasures of living with you forever. – Psalm 16:11 (NLT)

Sometimes claiming it verifies it in our hearts and minds.

Define the privilege of being able to invite God in to any area, circumstance, relationship, situation in your life. What does it mean to you that as a follower of Christ, you get to invite God in? Write your thoughts below.

_____

_____

_____

_____

What if you saw inviting God in as a privilege and not a requirement?

_____

_____

_____

_____

Now, let's look at the POWER of inviting God into our lives from the vantage point of our flesh and the vantage point of grace.

My flesh says:

O God *can't* really make that big of a difference, can He?

O God *won't* change anything too significantly.

O What can God do that hasn't *already been done* in this situation?

Grace says:

O *Nothing* is impossible with God.

O God can do *more* than I can even imagine.

O I can do *all* things through Christ.

Circle the statements above that your soul agrees with the most today.

Now all glory to God, who is able, through his mighty power at work within us, to accomplish infinitely more than we might ask or think. – Ephesians 3:20 (NLT)

What if you invited the power of God into your most difficult circumstances today? What might that look like? Jot down your thoughts below, and take a minute to pray and invite God into those circumstances.

_____

_____

_____

_____

Are you underestimating the impact God can have in your life? He can't do more than we can imagine if we haven't even invited Him to the party. What are you waiting for?

Invite Him in and watch Him work.

Enough leaving Him out. More inviting Him in.

He can't do more than we can imagine if we haven't even invited Him to the party.

ENOUGH SAID: AFTER READING TODAY'S lesson, let's capture a truth and take a step in obedience.

What did you hear God specifically say to you today through His Word?

_____

_____

_____

_____

How will you respond?

_____

_____

_____

_____

Fancy Pants Planning

For I know the plans I have for you, says the Lord. "They are plans for good and not for disaster, to give you a future and a hope.

– Jeremiah 29:11 (NLT)

I'M A PLANNER. SOME MIGHT call me a "type-A freak show on wheels," but I prefer executive planner.

My life runs on spreadsheets, calendars (make that one BIG calendar), and list after list. Some view it as pathetic. *A spreadsheet timeline to follow on vacation? Yes, please!* Others (my fellow type-Aers) see it as pure genius.

Yes, I have a plan for everything.

Confession: it's exhausting.

I'm planning my life—practically living my life—*before* it even happens, down to the nittty-gritty details in most cases.

If reservations aren't made, I see no real reason to go to dinner.

A weekend getaway requires an hour-by-hour itinerary.

Christmas shopping is mapped out like a Blackhawk rescue mission.

Corporate events led by yours truly include a binder the size of Texas with itemized assignments for the team.

I. Can't. Stop. Planning.

My elaborate plans are created to fit my fancy-pants world, and truth be told, inviting God into these plans of mine is often an afterthought.

To my type-B, laid back sisters, just because you're "winging it" day-in-and-day-out, laughing at me and my spreadsheets, doesn't mean you get a pass on today's lesson. #LoveYouMeanIt

Whether you're a planner extraordinaire or a fly-by-the-seat-of-your-pants kind of gal, your life has an agenda, and the King of Kings is waiting to be added to the schedule of events that is your life.

The book of Jonah packs a punch for us a today, so let's dig in and see what the Word has for us. Read Jonah (the entire book is only four short chapters. You got this!).

This book has so much we could chase after today, but let's stick to the script of inviting God in and do a quick analysis of the tug-of-war between Jonah's plans and God's lesson for him.

God's instruction for Jonah was well-defined.

> The Lord gave this message to Jonah son of Amittai: "Get up and go to the great city of Nineveh. Announce my judgment against it because I have seen how wicked its people are."

> But Jonah got up and went in the opposite direction to get away from the Lord. He went down to the port of Joppa, where he found a ship leaving for Tarshish. He bought a ticket and went on board, hoping to escape from the Lord by sailing to Tarshish.

> But the Lord hurled a powerful wind over the sea, causing a violent storm that threatened to break the ship apart. – Jonah 1:1-4 (NLT)

Right off the bat, the Lord is crystal clear on what He wants Jonah to do, and yet Jonah goes in the opposite direction.

Have you ever felt compelled by God to take a step in obedience, but ignored it, or even did exactly the opposite? Think about this, and jot down some examples below.

_____

_____

_____

_____

Has God given you clear instructions recently regarding a step of obedience? Write what the Lord is compelling you to do

_____

_____

_____

_____

Jonah recognized the outcome was on him.

"Throw me into the sea," Jonah said, "and it will become calm again. I know that this terrible storm is all my fault." – Jonah 1:12 (NLT)

Jonah knows the storm he and the sailors are battling is because he turned his back on the plans the Lord had for him.

Ignoring the Lord's plans for us has consequences. Have you ever found yourself in the middle of a storm that you created? If so, list the circumstances below.

_____

_____

_____

_____

Are there areas of your life where you are ignoring the Lord's prompts today? List these below and prayerfully reconsider the Lord's instruction.

_____

_____

_____

_____

The Lord grants second chances.

Then the Lord spoke to Jonah a second time: "Get up and go to the great city of Nineveh, and deliver the message I have given you."

> This time Jonah obeyed the Lord's command and went to Nineveh,
> a city so large that it took three days to see it all. – Jonah 3:1-3 (NLT)

Thankfully when we manufacture plans that don't include the Lord and His direction in our lives, mercy prevails. We serve a God who believes in do-overs.

Do you need a do-over today? Take a few minutes and boldly approach the throne of grace. Confess your disobedience, repent, and invite God into the circumstance(s). Document your prayer below.

_____

_____

_____

_____

_____

Obedience inspires God's favor.

> When God saw what they had done and how they had put a stop
> to their evil ways, he changed his mind and did not carry out the
> destruction he had threatened. – Jonah 3:10 (NLT)

I love the first phrase of this verse, "When God saw what they had done . . ."

Has it been a minute since God has seen what you have done for His Kingdom, or is God sitting back smiling at what you have recently done?

I've had my fair share of kingdom wins (woo hoo!), but I've also unloaded buckets full of do-overs and royal screw ups. If you're hitting it out of the park chasing after Him in full-out, wild surrender with all you possess, you go girl! But if yesterday was not your best day, and while you didn't find yourself in the mouth of a giant fish, that bed you're lying in is mighty uncomfortable—been there, done that, sister!

Mercy wins. Grace wins. Jesus wins.

Let's say enough to ignoring God's plans for us, and cling to the promise that Jesus Christ is more than enough for an eternity of do-overs. We are a work in progress.

For God is working in you, giving you the desire and the power to do what pleases him. – Philippians 2:13 (NLT)

Inviting God into our lives isn't a checklist, but an all-inclusive surrender of our meticulous plans.

Enough leaving Him out. More inviting Him in.

Inviting God into our lives isn't a checklist but an all-inclusive surrender of our meticulous plans.

ENOUGH SAID: AFTER READING TODAY'S lesson, let's capture a truth and take a step in obedience.

What did you hear God specifically say to you today through His Word?

_____

_____

_____

_____

How will you respond?

_____

_____

_____

_____

The Whole Pizza

The thief's purpose is to steal and kill and destroy. My purpose is to give them a rich and satisfying life.

– John 10:10 (NLT)

I WAS A YOUTH GROUP girl. That happy, sappy teenager twirling through life throwing out tracts like candy and inviting all my friends to church. Raise your hand if you owned the "Bo Knows Jesus" t-shirt. #SorryNotSorry

Hindsight: I was definitely less effective for the Kingdom than I thought I was, and I'm sure I offended many along the way with my Jesus-freak ways. By grace I pray someone saw through my naiveté and actually walked in to a relationship with Jesus.

It was my junior year of high school, and up until that point I was pretty certain I had this serving Jesus thing in the bag. I went to church every time the doors opened, mainly because Mom volunteered for just about everything at the church. I got that warm and fuzzy feeling at least once a month during a service, and I opened the Word at least once a week. I even had some verses underlined in my hunter green leather bound Bible with my name embossed on the front.

I was a Jesus girl through and through—or so I thought.

I had the best youth pastor. We called him Brother Sam, because that was the proper way we referred to our pastors at the Southern Baptist Church I attended growing up. He and his wife were so committed to us and our hearts, and I am so grateful that he showed me early on in my life that following Jesus was fun. I could write for days on all that Bro. Sam taught me, but one Sunday night service in particular sticks out most.

It was a lesson about pizza—a simple analogy that stopped me dead in my tracks.

"Your life is like a pizza," he said. "Every piece should belong to Jesus."

The combination of the Holy Spirit and the fact that I can connect with food analogies so well (bring on the pizza!), held so much weight for me on this particular night. I sat in that metal folding chair at Mt. Carmel Baptist Church in Cabot, Arkansas, and I was completely undone. The questions in my head began swirling.

You mean going to church isn't enough?

I handed out five tracts in English class yesterday, that's a win, right?

I brought three friends with me tonight. Doesn't that count for at least one piece of pizza?

What do you mean the whole pizza?

Piece by piece, Bro. Sam walked us through what it meant to surrender it all to Jesus—to invite Him in to every area of my life. I had one, maybe two pieces of the pizza devoted to Jesus, but there were so many things in my life I was idolizing more than Him.

Peter experienced a similar moment in the presence of Jesus. It wasn't a pepperoni parable, but an even better reminder that Christ alone should be our focus. Let's take a look:

> Six days later Jesus took Peter and the two brothers, James and John, and led them up a high mountain to be alone. As the men watched, Jesus' appearance was transformed so that his face shone like the sun, and his clothes became as white as light. Suddenly, Moses and Elijah appeared and began talking with Jesus.
>
> Peter exclaimed, "Lord, it's wonderful for us to be here! If you want, I'll make three shelters as memorials—one for you, one for Moses, and one for Elijah."
>
> But even as he spoke, a bright cloud overshadowed them, and a voice from the cloud said, "This is my dearly loved Son, who brings me great joy. Listen to him." The disciples were terrified and fell face down on the ground.
>
> Then Jesus came over and touched them. "Get up," he said. "Don't be afraid." And when they looked up, Moses and Elijah were gone, and they saw only Jesus. – Matthew 17:1-8 (NLT)

In our pizza of life, what are we holding equal to or even in higher regard than Jesus? Let's map it out and fill in some blanks by answering the questions below.

Time:

When it comes to how I spend my time, what is replacing Jesus?

_____

_____

_____

_____

What barriers or sin need to be removed to make room for Jesus in how I spend my time?

_____

_____

_____

_____

Finances:

When it comes to how I spend money, what am I idolizing over the Kingdom? Am I committed to regular tithes and offerings?

_____

_____

_____

What barriers or sin need to be removed to make room for Jesus in how I spend money?

_____

_____

_____

Habits:

When it comes to my habits, what is replacing Jesus?

_____

_____

_____

_____

What barriers or sin need to be removed to make room for Jesus relating to my habits?

_____

_____

_____

_____

Relationships:

When it comes to my relationships, have I invited Jesus in to all of my relationships?

_____

_____

_____

_____

What barriers or sin need to be removed to make room for Jesus in specific relationships I have? Do I desire a relationship with Jesus more than anyone else?

_____

_____

_____

_____

Work:

When it comes to my work outside and/or inside the home, what am I idolizing over Jesus?

_____

_____

_____

_____

Am I sharing Jesus at work? What barriers or sin need to be removed to make room for more of Jesus at work?

_____

_____

_____

_____

The same night I realized I had high-jacked nearly my entire pizza of life, I also realized I was more concerned with what God could give me than actually wanting more of God. My youth group girl shenanigans were really for my glory, not His.

Before we wrap up today, let's declare a shift in power in the tug-of-war between what the world can provide for our glory and the abundance of God when we give Him all the glory.

> For the Lord God is our sun and our shield. He gives us grace and glory. The Lord will withhold no good thing from those who do what is right. O Lord of Heaven's Armies, what joy for those who trust in you. – Psalm 84:11-12 (NLT)

It's time to invite God in to every piece of you. No one compares. Nothing matters more.

Enough leaving Him out. More inviting Him in.

Let's declare a shift in power in the tug-of-war between what the world can provide for our glory and the abundance of God when we give Him all the glory.

ENOUGH SAID: AFTER READING TODAY'S lesson, let's capture a truth and take a step in obedience.

What did you hear God specifically say to you today through His Word?

_____

_____

_____

_____

How will you respond?

_____

_____

_____

_____

Planting Seeds at the Post Office

Jesus replied, "You must love the Lord your God with all your heart, all your soul, and all your mind."

– Matthew 22:37 (NLT)

MY HUSBAND HAS THE GIFT of connection. He can connect with anyone in about two seconds: with a laugh, a smile, a funny story, a simple gesture. He has the ability to draw people in even if they don't know him.

There are downsides to this. We rarely go to any establishment where he doesn't know someone. He has friends for days. And, he will not put into practice the "if I don't look over they won't see me" trick—even when we're in a hurry. #Guilty

It is both lovely and exhausting to hang with him, and I'm pretty high on the extrovert scale! He's like a politician with his hand-shakin' and baby-kissin', and some days I can't hang.

What I love most about this man of mine, is that every connection he makes is purposeful. It's driven by his love for Christ and his passion for telling his world about Jesus in the everyday moments of his everyday life.

When we were dating, I was just beginning to deeply feel the tug on my heart for meaningful mission in my life. I remember having a conversation with him that went something like this (I might have been on the verge of a good ugly cry):

Me: *I feel like God wants me to do something, and I don't know exactly what it is. Nothing in my life actually matters. I'm busting my tail at this job, and it has no eternal value. I'm so confused. What do you think God is trying to tell me?*

Coby: *I think you're overcomplicating it a little.*

Me: *Of course you do!* (Cue the ugly cry.)

167

Coby: *I sell stamps, right? It's pretty simple, but I feel like God is using me to have eternal impact right where I am. I honor Him, glorify Him, and lead people to Him exactly where He puts me. And, today, I'm selling stamps in a small post office in North Little Rock, Arkansas.*

Me: <silence>

Coby understands full well that he is called to produce fruit where God puts him. He invites God in to every nook and cranny of his life, the obvious and the murky areas of life. The connections he makes with people are planted seeds that hopefully lead to a full harvest.

As we wrap up this week, let's look at one of the parables Jesus told and see what we can learn about seeds and the harvest.

Read Matthew 13:3-9.

Now, let's look at Jesus' explanation:

> "Now listen to the explanation of the parable about the farmer planting seeds: The seed that fell on the footpath represents those who hear the message about the Kingdom and don't understand it. Then the evil one comes and snatches away the seed that was planted in their hearts. The seed on the rocky soil represents those who hear the message and immediately receive it with joy. But since they don't have deep roots, they don't last long. They fall away as soon as they have problems or are persecuted for believing God's word. The seed that fell among the thorns represents those who hear God's word, but all too quickly the message is crowded out by the worries of this life and the lure of wealth, so no fruit is produced. The seed that fell on good soil represents those who truly hear and understand God's word and produce a harvest of thirty, sixty, or even a hundred times as much as had been planted!" – Matthew 13:18-23 (NLT)

The four types of seeds Jesus references don't require us to put ourselves in one category. Matter of fact, I think I've been in each of these categories at one point or another, maybe even at the same time depending on the area of my life.

I believe whether or not we have fertile soil that produces fruit in our lives, is directly tied to our posture and position related to Jesus. Hang with me here for a bit.

1. **Seed on the footpath: Those who hear the message, but don't understand it.**

Sometimes we're not listening. If we aren't positioned to hear God clearly, how can we expect Him to work through us?

List one adjustment you can make to better position yourself to hear God more clearly.

_____

2. **Seed on the rocky soil: Those who hear the message, immediately receive it with joy, but it doesn't last long.**

This is me on Sunday morning when I leave my row at church on fire, ready to speak life into everyone I encounter. And before I hit the door I've been invited to ride on the gossip train, so my ticket is punched and I'm more concerned with chatting it up *about* others instead of actually reaching them. This isn't a position that honors God or leads people to Jesus.

When you receive God and His message with joy, where/how/when do you get off track? Make note of the common barriers you run in to below, and list steps to remove them.

_____

_____

_____

3. **Seed among the thorns: Those who hear God's word, but the message is crowded out.**

I hang out here more often than I care to admit.

> The message is crowded out by the worries of this life and the lure of wealth, so no fruit is produced (v. 22).

Ouch! Painful, but true.

Friends, if you find yourself here from time to time, let's surrender our worry and desire for stuff that will never fulfill us. I think the answer for the worries of life and the wealth and status we crave is an invitation for more of Jesus.

What areas of your life could God invade and minimize your worry, anxiety, and need for more? List those areas below and write a prayer asking God to invade those areas of your life and remove your worry and empty cravings.

_____

_____

_____

4. Seed on good soil: Those who truly hear and understand God's Word and produce a harvest.

I want to live here. When God is invited in to all of me, I'm positioned to respond to His messages to my heart. That's when the fruit comes.

As we've journeyed through this idea of inviting God into our lives this week, what is the core message your heart is hearing from Him?

_____

_____

_____

The harvest comes where seeds are planted. The question is, what are we planting?

> You will always harvest what you plant. Those who live only to satisfy their own sinful nature will harvest decay and death from that sinful nature. But those who live to please the Spirit will harvest everlasting life from the Spirit. – Galatians 6:7-8 (NLT)

As we wrap up this week, consider the impact of inviting God into every area of your life.

O Let's remember He is the main character.

O Let's be careful not to underestimate God's impact in our lives.

O Let's say yes to God's plans for us.

O Let's position ourselves to hear His message so we can produce a harvest.

What would happen if we invited God into our homes, our businesses, our marriages, and our friendships? It's time to find out.

The harvest comes where seeds are planted. The question is, what are we planting?

ENOUGH SAID: AFTER READING TODAY'S lesson, let's capture a truth and take a step in obedience.

What did you hear God specifically say to you today through His Word?

_____

_____

_____

_____

How will you respond?

_____

_____

_____

_____

Let's say enough to leaving God out of our lives.

Extend the invitation.

Enough leaving Him out. More inviting Him in.

Enough of me. More of Jesus.

Week 6:

Enough *emptiness*. More PURPOSE.

And we know that God causes everything to work together for the good of those who love God and are called according to his purpose for them.

– Romans 8:28 (NLT)

A COUPLE OF YEARS AGO we did this exercise in time management at the office. In an effort to get a good glimpse at what is taking up our time, everyone at the advertising agency where I work was tasked with keeping a log of every minute in our day. Every. Single. Minute.

As you can imagine, there were moans and groans associated with this exercise. We begrudgingly completed the review of how we spent every moment of our work day, and let me tell you, it was painful. But, it was also revealing. The result was lessons learned and shifts in how we manage our work life.

Almost ninety minutes a day writing words that I could hand off to a copywriter: *yes please!*

Hours on conference calls: *don't schedule an hour call if you need only fifteen minutes.*

Emails have hijacked our entire work day: *for the love, don't cc me if it doesn't affect me.*

Once it was all said and done, I think I shaved off a good hour or two from my typical day in return for more productivity and a much happier work life. The exercise in identifying some of the emptiness holding my work day hostage was a little brutal, but the outcome was worth it.

Emptiness can creep in every category of life, providing hurdles to our purpose and mission.

This week, we're going to dive into this same type of exercise. I promise I have not included a timeline spreadsheet in this Bible Study for you to document every waking moment of your life. But, we are going to explore and hunt down any emptiness that is filling the gaps in our life.

Emptiness can creep in every category of life, providing hurdles to our purpose and mission. A good starting point in analyzing the emptiness that might be holding us back from our mission is to ask ourselves some questions.

What am I chasing?

How do I spend my time?

What consumes my thoughts?

Where and how do I spend my money?

How we answer these questions paints a pretty clear picture of what we're committed to, where our treasure is and what we're really pursuing.

If we're not careful, emptiness can take up some pretty hefty square feet in our lives. If I'm honest, I'm a professional at making room for all sorts of silliness that ultimately fits into the category of emptiness.

Four more episodes of my latest Netflix binge: *let's do this!*

Beach vacay or mission trip? *Toes in the sand for the win!*

Two-hour phone calls with my bestie chatting it up about you know who: *don't we just love a ride on the gossip train?*

Hours I spend trolling instastories vs. hours I spend in the Word. #TooCloseToCall

Now, let's hit the brakes for just a hot minute, take a breath, and recognize the balance that is living an abundant life with purpose and on mission. We checked out this verse back in week two, but let's digest this goodness one more time.

Seek the Kingdom of God above all else, and live righteously, and he will give you everything you need. – Matthew 6:33 (NLT)

We are called to seek the Kingdom of God above all else. With the Holy Spirit as our guide, we can navigate through decisions, choices, and all things meaningful and purposeful to bring glory to Him.

Chasing after Jesus is fun. Seeking the Kingdom of God is full of joy and goodness on every level. It's where Netflix binges play a part, but don't consume us. Beach vacays are on the agenda, but not the main focus of all our free time. Big laughs for the best instastories are big fun without derailing our time with God. And gossip sessions with our bestie are exchanged for speaking life into one another and encouraging lives on mission.

Seeking the Kingdom of God is over-the-top cool and exciting in every way possible. But, we'll never experience it as long as we're filling the gaps with emptiness.

My prayer for this week is that we hunt down the emptiness that stands between where we are today and where God wants to take us to fulfill our purpose in His Kingdom. I pray we find answers to questions that pierce our souls.

What does my life look like when I'm seeking the Kingdom of God?

What are the characteristics of righteous living for me?

What am I putting before the Kingdom of God, and whatever that is, does it even really matter?

This week, let's dig in and analyze Scripture that calls us to make room for purpose and stop pursuing all that doesn't matter for everything that does.

Enough emptiness. More purpose.

Hashtags, Hair Color, & Having it All Together

Since you have been raised to new life with Christ, set your sights on the reali-
ties of heaven, where Christ sits in the place of honor at God's right hand.
Think about the things of heaven, not the things of earth.

– Colossians 3:1-2 (NLT)

ONE FRIDAY MORNING NOT LONG ago, I sat at my kitchen table, Bible open, a blank page of my journal staring back at me, and tears running down my face. My husband stumbled in and went straight to the coffee pot like he does most mornings as he wipes away his eye crunchies in anticipation of his morning cup of joe.

He muttered, *"What is wrong? Are you crying at six a.m.?"*

Yes I was.

"Why?" He asked.

I had no idea. All I could muster up was: *I'm exhausted.*

The day, the week, the month ahead of me was too hard to wrap my head around. My full plate runneth over, and I had reached a breaking point.

Responsibilities and deadlines at work.

The kids and their schedules.

A bank account in the red.

A ministry checklist I am not checking off as quickly as I should.

Gray roots for days.

Two double-booked nights this weekend with a 100% chance someone's feelings will be hurt.

Seventeen text messages I haven't read or returned.

177

Laundry, party of five.

I was wedged between who I declared myself to be and the demands of being that person. Clearly I didn't measure up to the identity of the woman I was striving to be. You know, the girl with the perfect job. The perfect house. The perfect marriage. The perfect body. The perfect ministry. The perfect kids. The perfect life.

I was on the brink and there wasn't much one more day of dry shampoo and a dozen Frappuccino could do for me.

I was building a calendar and a schedule full of over-commitment.

Manufacturing a status I would never achieve.

Growing a savings account that would never be enough.

Constructing a career I would never be able to sustain at the pace I was going.

Encouraging fruitless friendships so I got all the invitations that put me on the RSVP list I had always admired.

I was chasing emptiness, and I was exhausted my friend.

Confession: I'm still exhausted most days. I wish I could tell you that Friday morning breaking point turned into an actual breakthrough, but the Holy Spirit won't let me lie and cover up this shattered identity of mine that rears its ugly head from time to time.

I wish we were having one of those Frappuccino together today. I would look you in the eye and ask, *"Are you exhausted, too? Are you chasing after the girl you want to be instead of being who God made you to be?"*

Can we say enough to this emptiness once and for all? Because there's not enough blood pressure medicine and Kleenex to get me through if I don't. And, we've got work to do—work that matters.

I say we go back to the basics with a reminder of exactly who we are.

Check the box if you agree with the following:

O **God is good.**

> Praise the Lord! Give thanks to the Lord, for He is good! His faithful love endures forever. – Psalm 106:1 (NLT)

I'm pretty sure if you picked up this Bible study, you probably agree on some level that God is good. You might even add a bold "all the time." Check that box if you agree!

O **I am made in the image of God.**

> So God created human beings in his own image. In the image of God he created them; male and female he created them. – Genesis 1:27 (NLT)

If you agree with Genesis 1:27, then you agree that you were made in the image of God. Put a check in the box if you're still with me.

O **I'm messed up. I'm a sinner.**

> For everyone has sinned; we all fall short of God's glorious standard. – Romans 3:23 (NLT)

Adam and Eve led the way to our sinful nature, but we have all fallen short of God's glory and goodness. Check that box sister – it's a fact.

O **Because of Jesus, I am made new.**

> Yes, Adam's one sin brings condemnation for everyone, but Christ's one act of righteousness brings a right relationship with God and new life for everyone. – Romans 5:18 (NLT)

Jesus made a way, paid all my debt, and provides a pathway back to goodness for me. Hallelujah for this check mark!

Maybe you're not struggling with face plants at your kitchen table, and you've worked through these faulty identity struggles. Amen to that! But a quick review never hurt a girl, so humor those of us who need a reminder of who we are every now and then. Let's bring this all home with some truth and assurance in who we are in Christ.

If we believe that God is good, that means we know for sure that we are good, because we were made in the image of God.

Yes, we messed it up with our sin, but Jesus changed everything.

My identity is in Christ, not in the identity of the woman I'm chasing after. God didn't make us to chase after an identity we're not. He made us in His image, for His Kingdom, to live out His purpose.

If we know these things for sure, what the heck happened? When did we end up at our kitchen table weeping over hashtags, hair color, and having it all together?

It's time to dig deep, pull ourselves out of the pit of emptiness, and walk in the identity of being made new in the goodness of God.

Are you wedged between who you think you have to be and who you really are?

If yes, what are you striving and believing you have to earn, accomplish, complete, or be that is creating brokenness in your identity? Pray through your list individually, and ask God to remove each piece of brokenness from your identity and replace it with the truth of who you are in Him. Fill in the space below, I've started a list—add your own.

Lies of Brokenness in My Identity　　　**Truth of Who I am in Christ**

A full calendar means a full life.　　　I am only full in life when I'm full in Christ.

_____

_____

_____

_____

_____

Whether you're wrestling with large chunks of lies and brokenness in your identity, or small bits of shattered identity, standing firm in who we are in Christ contradicts our culture and the world's standards.

The gospel compels us to focus on the Kingdom of God and not what the world tells us is important. We get to concentrate on investing in the next generation, making disciples, building meaningful relationships that lead to life change, and glorifying God in our everyday moments.

Instead of focusing on the emptiness we're chasing, what can you focus on that speaks life into your identity in Christ? Jot down some thoughts below on what you get to focus on because you're a daughter of Christ.

_____

_____

_____

_____

We are His daughters, called to chase after purpose not emptiness.

It is God who enables us, along with you, to stand firm for Christ. He has commissioned us, and he has identified us as his own by placing the Holy Spirit in our hearts as the first installment that guarantees everything he has promised us. – 2 Corinthians 21-22 (NLT)

We are His own, rescued by Jesus and measured by His grace alone. Our identity in Christ drives our purpose, not chasing after someone we were never meant to be.

Enough emptiness. More purpose.

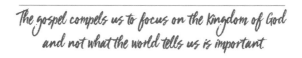

The gospel compels us to focus on the Kingdom of God and not what the world tells us is important.

ENOUGH SAID: AFTER READING TODAY'S lesson, let's capture a truth and take a step in obedience.

What did you hear God specifically say to you today through His Word?

_____

_____

_____

_____

How will you respond?

_____

_____

_____

_____

Manufacturing Purpose

If you look for me wholeheartedly, you will find me.

– Jeremiah 29:13 (NLT)

GROWING UP ALL I WANTED to be was Katie Couric. I wanted to live in front of the camera on weekday mornings in Rockefeller Center telling stories on national television while others drank their coffee and tuned in to the *Today Show*.

I had it all mapped out. When I went to college, I immediately declared my major Mass Communications and headed down the path of becoming Katie's replacement, or so I dreamed. Then, after my sophomore year of college, I took an internship at a local television station.

My first week I was reprimanded for placing the teleprompter script on the director's board (a big no-no!). Papers flew everywhere as the director swiped the script off his board so he could do his job. I learned cuss words I had never heard before, and most of them were targeted at me and the train wreck that I was in the control room.

It wasn't long before I was "re-assigned" from the control room to the newsroom. But wait, *I'm certain Katie doesn't work in the newsroom*, she's much closer to the control room and the Holy Grail—the actual studio.

I quickly found my stride in the newsroom and actually began to excel. I called my parents every night a story would air that I wrote.

Mom, the OJ Simpson update—I wrote every word that reporter said!

Formulating stories, scheduling interviews, and tasking cameramen and crew to the day's assignment was my jam. But I was convinced Katie never spent a hot minute in the newsroom or serving as the "grip" on a shoot holding camera wire for days.

183

So, when I went back to college for my junior year, I quickly changed my schedule to include a Television Production class. I was determined to rock that control room next summer. This class would help me score an internship with on-camera talent at a TV station, and I would begin making my way up to my dream of morning show stardom.

It turns out Television Production class is not a cakewalk. It included math, equipment I had never seen in my life, math, a syllabus that would scare even a type-A overachiever, more math, and curriculum that appeared to include engineering on some level. #IDontDoMath

Needless to say, I dropped Television Production like a hot potato and replaced it with a Public Relations Strategy class that was right up my alley, and the rest is history.

For decades I was manufacturing my future career. Everywhere I turned doors were slamming in my face, but my determination to be on television ran deep. Not until I finally found a home on the Advertising Federation Team, with an "A" in Feature Writing and encouragement from my professors in Public Relations did I resign my dream of television and cross over to the other side, advertising.

Twenty years later, this career in advertising and marketing has been filled with favor and fun, and I still love it every day. Something tells me I would still be clawing my way through television production had I continued to feed that obsession.

This inclination to manufacture my life based on my own agenda is a common theme, and my walk with Christ is no exception. I have to be cautious that I'm not manufacturing my purpose in the Kingdom of God, and instead focus on remaining and abiding in Him.

A couple of weeks ago, when we were navigating through the distractions that stand in the way of our mission, we dialed up John fifteen. And, we're going right back there today, but let's pick up where we left off. Remember, Jesus is hanging out with the disciples outlining some super important stuff.

Read John 15:5-12.

There is so much goodness here we could tackle, but today let's focus on the words of Jesus in verses five and six:

> "Yes, I am the vine; you are the branches. Those who remain in me, and I in them, will produce much fruit. For apart from me you can do nothing. Anyone who does not remain in me is thrown away like a useless branch and withers. Such branches are gathered into a pile to be burned." – John 15:5-6 (NLT)

Remember, we identified that Jesus is the vine and the fruit is our mission—the possibility of what our life can produce for the Kingdom and for His glory. Today, let's take it a step further and recognize the seed of that fruit.

The precursor to the fruit of mission is remaining in Him. Many translations use the word *abide* instead of *remain*, meaning to dwell, to stay, to settle in, to sink deeper.

Our purpose comes alive when we remain in Jesus—when we dwell in Him—sinking deeper in His ways.

I spend a hefty amount of time in women's ministry, and I hear from ladies on the regular about all things purpose, and God's will, and . . . *if I just knew what God wanted me to do!* The Holy Spirit always brings me back to these verses in John fifteen as my go-to response to these inquiries on the discernment of purpose and God's will.

We might be thirsty for purpose because we're not remaining in the One who defines it all for us.

Can you describe a time in your life when you were remaining and abiding in Him? What does it look like for you to remain (or abide) in Christ?

_____

_____

_____

_____

Now, let's do a quick evaluation on where we are today in our "remaining and abiding" efforts. What are some practical steps you can commit to to sink in deeper in your relationship with Christ?

_____

_____

_____

_____

Take a few minutes and pray a prayer of commitment over these steps you've listed. Ask God to remind you of these action items and provide accountability in your spirit.

Steps of commitment to abiding in Him are fruitful, and we have to be careful of the emptiness around us that creeps in and locks down our faithfulness.

There are days when I'm running faster to my Facebook feed than I am to the Word of God, and I'm wondering why I don't understand God's will. Abiding and remaining in Jesus is not a destination, it's a process of persistence. It's a commitment to declaring the gospel as the anthem of our lives and bidding farewell to the world's standards.

> Do not love this world nor the things it offers you, for when you love the world, you do not have the love of the Father in you. – 1 John 2:15 (NLT)

My days aren't measured by how many likes I get on Facebook, it's a new value system. Jesus is the benchmark for purpose in our lives.

Enough emptiness. More purpose.

We might be thirsty for purpose because we're not remaining in the One who defines it all for us.

ENOUGH SAID: AFTER READING TODAY'S lesson, let's capture a truth and take a step in obedience.

What did you hear God specifically say to you today through His Word?

_____

_____

_____

_____

How will you respond?

_____

_____

_____

_____

The High Cost of Chasing Emptiness

*So we are Christ's ambassadors; God is making his appeal through us. We
speak for Christ when we plead, "Come back to God!"*

– 2 Corinthians 5:20 (NLT)

IS IT BAD THAT I love to see church-folk squirm a little? I don't know why,
but I love when pastors teeter on the edge of our comfort zones, and the room
gets a little itchy on Sundays.

My pastor is that guy.

He never disappoints, and I'm so grateful I get to hear Pastor Scott Harness
pour into me and my family, challenging us out of our comfort zones every
week at That.Church in Sherwood, Arkansas.

A couple of weeks ago he got me. There I sat, eleven rows back at the ten
a.m. service. I was laughing through the sermon, filling in the blanks of my
outline like a type-A boss, and then he blurted out, "It ought to be really hard
for the people around you to go to hell."

What the wha?!

I repeated it back to myself over and over, and suddenly felt the ugly cry
swelling up inside me. *Is it really hard to be around me and go to hell?*

The cost of this emptiness we're chasing is high. Eternities are at stake. I
know it sounds heavy and uncomfortable or maybe even difficult, but y'all,
it's time for a gut check. Is the emptiness we're chasing gambling eternities?

Think about the people you encounter frequently and have influence on,
and then list them in the column on the left (even if you can't list them by
name, *i.e. the girl at the check-out counter at the cleaners*). Now, on the right, put

a **check mark** next to the ones you are intentionally investing in their eternity and place an **X** next to the ones you doubt even know you're a believer. (Include groups of people when applicable, i.e. "baseball moms at the ballpark," or "coworkers," etc.).

People You Encounter/Influence	X or ✓

The emptiness we're chasing is replacing purpose in our lives. Purpose leads to mission and mission leads to people coming to know Christ.

Check out this great reminder from Jesus of what it looks like to hold on to emptiness.

Once a religious leader asked Jesus this question: "Good Teacher, what should I do to inherit eternal life?"

"Why do you call me good?" Jesus asked him. "Only God is truly good. But to answer your question, you know the commandments: 'You must not commit adultery. You must not murder. You must not steal. You must not testify falsely. Honor your father and mother.'"

The man replied, "I've obeyed all these commandments since I was young."

When Jesus heard his answer, he said, "There is still one thing you haven't done. Sell all your possessions and give the money to the poor, and you will have treasure in heaven. Then come, follow me."

But when the man heard this he became very sad, for he was very rich. – Luke 18:18-23 (NLT)

A question I have when I get to Heaven is whether or not this man would have become one of the disciples had he sold his possessions and followed Jesus. Would his life have resulted in a gazillion eternities rescued, or did he risk eternities by holding on to his worldly treasures?

Oh, how the Holy Spirit and I have wrestled over what I'm holding on to in this fancy-pants world.

For this man it was wealth, money, and possessions, but what emptiness are we holding on to? What is holding you back from rescuing eternities in your everyday life? Maybe it's a specific sin, a time stealer or two, shame, a status you're trying to uphold. I don't know what it is for you, but claim it and name it in the spaces below.

Now, take a few minutes and pray through these barriers to your purpose, and ask God to remove them from your heart, mind, and soul so you can shift your perspective.

There have been seasons in my life when I didn't consider the gravity of my influence. Without even realizing it, I was jeopardizing eternities. I grieve the souls that don't know Jesus because I was too busy holding on to emptiness in the form of my pride, fear, and just plain ole laziness.

I know that grace covers all of that nonsense, but it's a reminder that what I deem as important in any season of life fades in comparison to the value of knowing Jesus Christ and sharing Him with my world. We cannot underestimate the power of living out the gospel in our lives and sharing it with our world.

My current state of affairs doesn't dictate how or if I live out my purpose, but my perspective does. When we hold fast to what the world offers, it's easy for emptiness to hold our purpose hostage.

For the world offers only a craving for physical pleasure, a craving for everything we see, and pride in our achievements and possessions. These are not from the Father, but are from this world. – 1 John 2:16 (NLT)

What are you currently craving?

_____

_____

_____

_____

Beside each of the cravings you listed, put a "W" beside them if they're from the world and put an "F" beside them if they're from the Father.

Now, review your list and spend a few minutes in prayer removing those cravings from the world.

When we shift our perspective to have eternal impact, the emptiness that's consuming us seems silly, foolish, and reckless.

We're chasing after what the world has for us today when eternity is the prize and Jesus is the answer.

Enough emptiness. More purpose.

The cost of this emptiness we're chasing is high. Eternities are at stake.

ENOUGH SAID: AFTER READING TODAY'S lesson, let's capture a truth and take a step in obedience.

What did you hear God specifically say to you today through His Word?

_____

_____

_____

_____

How will you respond?

_____

_____

_____

_____

Legacy in the Leftovers

I tell you the truth, everyone who acknowledges me publicly here on earth, the Son of Man will also acknowledge in the presence of God's angels.

– Luke 12:8 (NLT)

YESTERDAY WE EVALUATED THE GRAVITY of the emptiness we chase, the cost of putting junk that just plain doesn't matter in front of the One who does. And while you might have been super-excited about turning the page and digging in to today's lesson after the heaviness of yesterday, stay with me, because we're going to hang out here for just a bit longer.

When we wrapped up yesterday, we were mourning the times in our lives when we were emptiness chasers (well, I can't speak for you, but I sure was!).

I will never get back those seasons of life when I was consumed by the insignificant. If I could go back and speak to twenty-something Priscilla, I would have a few words of wisdom for her:

O *That career you're running loud and proud after will not fulfill you, no matter how much money you make.*

O *Those good times you're chasing have consequences.*

O *The hours you're spending watching your DVR and Googling details about the Real Housewives are fruitless.*

O *Gossip isn't fun. It's painful and hurtful and divides hearts.*

I would tell her to stop chasing emptiness that will never be enough and start running after Jesus who will always and forever be more than enough.

Sadly, my twenty-something self isn't here to hear my words of wisdom. But, forty-two-year-old Priscilla is ready to see what God has for me on the other side. What will be my legacy in the leftovers after chasing emptiness for more years than I can count?

Whether you've been chasing emptiness for five minutes or five decades, we can be certain there is a legacy in all that is left of our lives here in this world. We have a purpose. God has a plan. And it's time to finish the work.

Let's look at one of my all-time favorite Scriptures.

Read John 4:1-30.

Now, let's read verses twenty-five to thirty again together.

> The woman said, "I know the Messiah is coming—the one who is called Christ. When he comes, he will explain everything to us."
>
> Then Jesus told her, "I am the Messiah!"
>
> Just then his disciples came back. They were shocked to find him talking to a woman, but none of them had the nerve to ask, "What do you want with her?" or "Why are you talking to her?" The woman left her water jar beside the well and ran back to the village, telling everyone, "Come and see a man who told me everything I ever did! Could he possibly be the Messiah?" So the people came streaming from the village to see him. – John 4:25-30 (NLT)

This infamous woman at the well had clearly been chasing some emptiness. She was trying to find her worth in husband after husband, and no tellin' what else.

And then she encountered Jesus.

The beauty of this story is that she didn't let the fact that she had been busy with all that nonsense for all those years hold her back for one second. She literally went running back to her village to tell everyone about Jesus.

She had a shift in her purpose after she looked the Messiah in the face, and she never looked back.

My sweet sisters, the life we have left is so much more than a pocket full of leftover years that might have a hint of purpose left. Every waking moment we have is an opportunity to run and tell our village about Jesus. And those opportunities start now.

Let's have our own woman at the well story right here on these pages. Let's take a minute and encounter Jesus with some sweet reminders to our soul.

1. His love for me is great – the cross proves it.

> But God showed his great love for us by sending Christ to die for us while we were still sinners. – Romans 5:8 (NLT)

Maybe emptiness shows up for you off and on, in one season, but not in all. Or maybe you struggle with the square footage the emptiness you're chasing takes up in your heart of hearts frequently. No matter your degree of emptiness, let's replace it with purpose by claiming the great love of Jesus Christ and the debt He paid for us.

2. The new me is righteous and holy because of Jesus.

> Throw off your old sinful nature and your former way of life, which is corrupted by lust and deception. Instead, let the Spirit renew your thoughts and attitudes. Put on your new nature, created to be like God—truly righteous and holy. – Ephesians 4:22-24 (NLT)

We do not give ourselves permission to live one more minute in the sinful nature of the emptiness we've chased in the past. The Spirit has renewed us. We can settle in His holiness.

3. He leads and guides me on the best pathway.

> The Lord says, "I will guide you along the best pathway for your life. I will advise you and watch over you. – Psalm 32:8 (NLT)

Not only does God have a plan and purpose for us, but He will equip us, guide us, and advise along the way. We can run to our villages and fulfill our purpose, and He will create the pathway.

My woman at the well story—my encounter with Jesus—is different than yours. My rescue and revival doesn't look like yours. The beauty of our Savior is the portraits He paints, story after story of what He has done in the lives of His daughters.

It's high time we tell our story.

But, we can't tell our village about our encounter with Jesus until we fundamentally understand it in our hearts. In the space below, write your testimony—your encounter with Jesus—in its simplest form.

_____

_____

_____

_____

_____

If you're struggling to tell your story, here are some questions to ask yourself:

What has God done in my life?

Has He rescued me from a storm?

Have I been delivered from pain or suffering?

Do I know for sure my life would be fundamentally different if Jesus never showed up on the scene?

Why?

How?

When we tell our story, hearts open and the floodgates of life change open.

Remember verse thirty in the story we read today? It reminds us of the impact of the gospel. After the woman at the well ran to her village, the Word says . . . *So the people came streaming from the village to see him (John 4:30).*

My prayer is that every soul reading these words will say enough to the emptiness holding you captive. I pray you will live out the purpose God has for you, and that the people in your villages and the places God has put you will come streaming to Him

> But Jesus said, "No, go home to your family, and tell them every-thing the Lord has done for you and how merciful he has been."
> – Mark 5:19 (NLT)

Our villages are waiting to hear about our encounter with Jesus. Let's say goodbye to the emptiness in our past and make purpose our present.

Enough emptiness. More purpose.

Every waking moment we have is an opportunity to run and tell our village about Jesus. And those opportunities start now.

ENOUGH SAID: AFTER READING TODAY'S lesson, let's capture a truth and take a step in obedience.

What did you hear God specifically say to you today through His Word?

_____

_____

_____

_____

How will you respond?

_____

_____

_____

_____

Hijacked Purpose

And whatever you do or say, do it as a representative of the Lord Jesus, giving thanks through him to God the Father.

– Colossians 3:17 (NLT)

WE HAVE AN ELF ON the Shelf. His name is Bill. I know it's weird and creepy and probably wrong on many levels, but there's no shame in my game when it comes to utilizing any tool available for parenting leverage.

For those of you who aren't moms or you don't indulge in mainstream silliness, an Elf on the Shelf is a fictitious elf that supposedly flies home to the North Pole every night during the Christmas season and tells Santa Claus all about your child's behavior. The elf is watching and everyone should be on their best behavior. #BeGoodForGoodnessSake

The first Christmas season Bill was with us, my three-year-old daughter hijacked his purpose. Instead of focusing on how *she* behaved and what Bill and Santa thought about that, she was focused on my husband's behavior, and she was compelled to notify Bill of his every wrong turn.

Bill, Daddy stole one of my Cheetos.

Bill, Daddy's chewing with his mouth open.

Bill, Daddy said a bad word!

And while I secretly loved every minute of it, my daughter had flipped the script on Bill and his purpose. She shifted our elf's purpose to fit her plans in her comfort zone. Bill didn't have time to focus on Stella when he was busy worrying about Daddy and his shenanigans.

As we wrap up this week of evaluating the role emptiness plays in our life, I wonder if we're letting emptiness hijack our purpose.

Read John 9:1-34.

This story has so many characters, and I don't know about you, but I can see myself in each of them.

1. The Pharisees

> Some of the Pharisees said, "This man Jesus is not from God, for he is working on the Sabbath." Others said, "But how could an ordinary sinner do such miraculous signs?" So there was a deep division of opinion among them. – John 9:16 (NLT)

Haven't we all been here? Searching. Full of unbelief. Divided. The Pharisees didn't know what they believed, but they questioned who Jesus was.

Name a time in your life when you questioned God and His purpose for your life. If you've been in this position, share that memory in the space below.

_____

_____

_____

2. The Parents

> The Jewish leaders still refused to believe the man had been blind and could now see, so they called in his parents. They asked them, "Is this your son? Was he born blind? If so, how can he now see?"

> His parents replied, "We know this is our son and that he was born blind, but we don't know how he can see or who healed him. Ask him. He is old enough to speak for himself." His parents said this because they were afraid of the Jewish leaders, who had announced that anyone saying Jesus was the Messiah would be expelled from the synagogue. That's why they said, "He is old enough. Ask him." – John 9:18-23 (NLT)

The blind man's parents knew Jesus had healed him, but they wanted no part of it. Their fear overshadowed their purpose.

Has there been a time in your life when you wanted no part of what God had for you—when your fear surpassed your purpose? If so, share the specifics of this time in your life below.

_____

_____

_____

3. The Blind Man

"I don't know whether he is a sinner," the man replied. "But I know this: I was blind, and now I can see!" – John 9:25 (NLT)

The blind man didn't fully understand why or how Jesus healed him, but he had faith in who Jesus was because he knew what He had done for him. He now had a testimony to tell of the healing power of Jesus.

What do you know for sure? Does your testimony include a story of faith that you might not understand how or why, but you know that it was only possible because of Jesus? Share your thoughts in the space below.

_____

_____

_____

Our purpose is rooted in what God has already done in our lives, in what we know for sure. If we ignore it, we're ignoring our purpose.

As God's partners, we beg you not to accept this marvelous gift of God's kindness and then ignore it. – 2 Corinthians 6:1 (NLT)

As daughters in Christ, we can't let emptiness hijack our purpose. We are called to the purpose God has for us, the purpose of seeking the Kingdom of God, making disciples, and glorifying Him every step of the way.

Whether emptiness has hijacked your purpose for one minute, one year, or one lifetime, it's far too long. As we wrap up this week, let's recap how we can replace emptiness with purpose once and for all.

○ Let's allow our identity in Christ to drive our purpose.

○ Let's remain in Him to quench our thirst for God's will in our lives.

○ Let's recognize the cost of chasing emptiness – our purpose leads to rescues for eternity.

○ Let's leave a legacy in the time we have left telling our villages about our encounter with Jesus.

Chasing emptiness is exhausting. Isn't it time to say enough to the junk that's consuming us and walk in the purpose God has for us?

As daughters in Christ we can't let emptiness hijack our purpose.

ENOUGH SAID: AFTER READING TODAY'S lesson, let's capture a truth and take a step in obedience.

What did you hear God specifically say to you today through His Word?

_____

_____

_____

_____

How will you respond?

_____

_____

_____

_____

It's time to tell the story of what we know for sure—a Savior paid it all, and our encounter with Jesus changed everything.

Enough emptiness. More purpose.

Enough of me. More of Jesus.

Week 7:

Enough *good intentions*. More BOLD OBEDIENCE.

If you love me, obey my commandments.

– John 14:15 (NLT)

I WAS PRAYING FOR A breakthrough, for God to show up in a mighty way. It had been my prayer for months, and I felt like everywhere I turned I was seeing God moving in the lives of people who had a common thread of obedience—fasting.

I had fasted before, either with my church body or simple fasts in small windows, but nothing too radical. If I wanted God to show up, I felt the tug on my heart to be bold in my chase after Him. For me, in the season I was in, fasting seemed bold.

The Holy Spirit and I had worked it all out. I would fast every Wednesday for ten weeks, drinking only water on those days and replacing food and snacks with prayer and focus on seeking His face. Wednesdays were the best days for me to fast undercover because my family all went our separate ways for school and work during the day and various ministries at church in the evenings. I could fast with humility, and only God and I would know.

My intentions were great.

The first Wednesday just so happened to land in a week where I was traveling for work. I was in Orlando for a conference. I hopped a plane early that morning to head to Tennessee for another conference where I had a speaking engagement. This particular Wednesday would be me traveling and then landing at the hotel to work and wrap up my day. Not a bad scenario to start a fast when I'm traveling alone.

Except that by eleven a.m. I fell on my face right in the middle of a Sonic value meal.

203

I had feared the lack of caffeine more than anything, but when I got off that plane at ten forty-five that morning after guzzling water the entire flight, somehow my rental car drove straight to the nearest drive thru. One value meal, one package of almond M&M's, a pizza for dinner and half a Twix bar later, the fast was definitely over. #EpicFail

Have you ever been clear on something God wanted you to do, and you had every intention of carrying it through, but then life happened and you found yourself with an empty cheeseburger wrapper in the floorboard of your rental car?

Good intentions say I'm just fine right here thank you very much, but bold obedience will rock our world. Reality is I rarely want anything to *really* rock my world unless it's an epic shoe sale, French fries without calories, or permanent hair color that promises no more gray roots.

Are we pretty comfortable in our Sunday pews and rows, with our verse-of-the-day and our goodnight prayers? Is it possible that we're so far down in the pit of good intentions that we can't comprehend what bold obedience even looks like in our world?

Hopefully not, but if we are, I pray this week we experience revival as daughters of Christ living out loud through bold steps of faith and obedience.

If you find yourself in the pit of good intentions from time to time, this week we're going to dig our way out.

As daughters in Christ, we have been given an assignment of obedience. The Great Commission instructs us to *go and make disciples*, but the follow-up is a declaration to teach obedience.

> Teach these new disciples to obey all the commands I have given you. And be sure of this: I am with you always, even to the end of the age. – Matthew 28:20 (NLT)

Teaching obedience requires obedience.

When it comes to the balance of grace and holiness, if I'm honest, I give grace the edge most days. Grace creates freedom and makes a way for the jacked up parts of me to find restoration. It's a reflection of the gospel that is beautiful and all-consuming. I'm in love with grace.

While I can't honestly say I'm painting holiness and obedience with the same strokes I'm painting grace, I can say that I'm discovering that chasing after God in full surrender is a privilege. When I shine bold obedience in the light of joy and opportunity, it compels me to be bolder, run faster, and leave my good intentions in the dust.

Grace and mercy reign in the life of a follower of Christ, but obedience is also critical to abundant living.

This week we're going to conduct an honest evaluation of our pursuit of holiness, and I pray the Holy Spirit will speak loud and clear into our hearts.

As you prepare for this week and all God has for us, let's evaluate where good intentions rule over bold obedience in our lives. Consider where you may have become complacent in your walk, content in where you are, and ask the Holy Spirit to identify areas where He's calling you beyond those good intentions.

Good intentions say I'm just fine right here thank you very much, but bold obedience will rock our world.

For me, it's the checklist. I check the box on everything I think a good Jesus girl should do, and hope I'm meeting the standard:

Pray every morning – check.

Read my Bible – check.

Go to church – check.

Don't cuss – check.

Tithe – check.

Serve in ministry – check.

It's a checklist of good intentions that if I'm not careful becomes a meaningless list of checkmarks with no real purpose and mission.

Your scuffle with good intentions might look different than mine, but let's take a few minutes and listen to what the Spirit has to say about the current state of our good intentions. Let's allow God to show us bold steps of obedience we can take this week. Because when bold obedience replaces good intentions, the ground will shake and mission comes alive in our hearts.

Enough checking the boxes.

Enough being just fine where we are.

Enough good intentions. More bold obedience.

How Do You Like Your Coffee?

And so the Lord says, "These people say they are mine. They honor me with their lips, but their hearts are far from me. And their worship of me is nothing but man-made rules learned by rote.

– Isaiah 29:13 (NLT)

DON'T TALK TO ME BEFORE I've had two cups of coffee in the morning. My family can attest to the fact that I'm a renegade before caffeine.

How do you like your coffee? Maybe you're hard core and take yours black. Or, maybe you're like me and enjoy a smidge of creamer and a packet of sweetener in your morning cup of joe. Maybe you're like my husband, and you prefer a little coffee with your cream and sugar. And, where are my Frappuccino girls at? Because coffee on ice is heaven with a little whip cream on top.

Every coffee drinker has their way, their cup of perfection. And if you don't drink coffee, I love you, but I don't get it.

I've seen all types of coffee drinkers, but never have I ever found someone who prefers their coffee lukewarm. That word lukewarm is so yucky, murky, and stale. It leaves a bad taste in my mouth just thinking about it.

Today we're going to take a look at this idea of being lukewarm, and we're hanging out in Revelation three where God has some pretty harsh words for the Church at Laodicea.

> "I know all the things you do, that you are neither hot nor cold. I wish that you were one or the other! But since you are like lukewarm water, neither hot nor cold, I will spit you out of my mouth! You say, 'I am rich. I have everything I want. I don't need a thing!' And you don't realize that you are wretched and miserable and poor and blind and naked." – Revelation 3:15-17 (NLT)

Talk about a mic drop. God is pretty clear in this letter to the Church at Laodicea about how He feels regarding where they are on the scale of hot and cold.

This Scripture is from one of the seven letters to the Churches in Revelation, and after studying about Laodicea, there are some interesting aspects of this area to point out. Laodicea was a very rich city, a place where they produced fine black wool, and they had a prestigious medical school. It was a happening place.

Laodicea was a tough place to get water, so they built aqueducts to bring water in to the city. They brought in cold water from the mountains in the north and hot water from the hot springs in the south, but once the water travelled through the aqueducts it was neither hot nor cold, it was lukewarm. The Laodicean church knew full well what God meant by lukewarm. Unfortunately, so do I.

I'm pretty darn good at being lukewarm in my walk with Christ. I've actually perfected the art of lukewarm Christianity. I even justify my "lukewarmness."

I go to church.
I went to the women's retreat last year.
I say prayers with my kids at night.
I read my devotional every day.
I know Jesus.

Please don't misunderstand me in defining my lukewarm state. All of these things are good—they're fantastic actually. The actions I'm taking are all good, but some days the mindset behind them might be a little off.

It's easy to create a destination of obedience instead of a continued progression of obedience. If I'm chasing after completing the catalog of obedience, I'll miss the reward in the evolution of surrender.

Bold obedience is a process not a destination.

Let's step back a minute and do a quick evaluation.

On the scale of hot and cold: hot being you are living your life in wild abandon chasing after God in full surrender, and cold being the dry place you've been for a while without any compulsion for Jesus, where do you fall today? Put an X on the scale below.

COLD ——————————————————————————— HOT

Now, think about what is standing between where you are today and the hotter end of the scale. Jot down some barriers that are making it difficult to be hot in your pursuit of God.

_____

_____

_____

_____

_____

What are some bold steps of obedience you can take to remove these barriers? List at least 3 below.

_____

_____

_____

_____

_____

I fell flat on my face when I went through these exercises recently. I prayed for some super-spiritual answer for what was standing between where I am in my lukewarm living and the desire in my heart to live out loud on the hot end of the scale chasing after God with everything I have. The answer the Holy Spirit gave me left me in a spiritual face plant.

It's you, Priscilla. You are why you're lukewarm. You are the barrier.

This face plant resulted in an assessment of my good intentions. I surrendered my destination of obedience, and committed to live in the progression of surrender. I'm dying to myself daily, and He's coming alive in me.

Have you made obedience a destination? Are you pursuing a checklist of do's and don'ts? Or, are you committed to the progress of becoming more like Jesus every day? Jot down your thoughts below.

_____

_____

_____

_____

After God rebukes the Church at Laodicea, He wraps up His letter with instructions to be diligent and repent, adding in the promise that He's always here, standing at the door and knocking.

> "Look! I stand at the door and knock. If you hear my voice and open the door, I will come in, and we will share a meal together as friends. Those who are victorious will sit with me on my throne, just as I was victorious and sat with my Father on his throne." – Revelation 3:19-21 (NLT)

As we do an honest evaluation of where we are on the scale of hot and cold, I'm confident God is asking us to open the door and hear His voice. I heard Him loud and clear as He reminded me that I'm in the way of all He has for me.

Maybe you're hearing Him too. Maybe He's asking you to take a step of obedience or to make more time for Him. Maybe He's asking you to trust Him in a specific area of your life, or drop a habit that is consuming you. I don't know what you're hearing Him say to you today, but I know that when we hear His knock and open the door, He comes in and everything changes.

Enough good intentions. More bold obedience.

I don't know what you're hearing Him say to you today, but I know that when we hear His knock and open the door, He comes in and everything changes.

ENOUGH SAID: AFTER READING TODAY'S lesson, let's capture a truth and take a step in obedience.

What did you hear God specifically say to you today through His Word?

_____

_____

_____

_____

How will you respond?

_____

_____

_____

_____

Simple Recipes to the Rescue

Jesus replied, "But even more blessed are all who hear the word of God and put it into practice."

– Luke 11:28 (NLT)

I'VE GOT SKILLS. A COUPLE of them, like decorating a Christmas tree in five minutes flat and rapping my 90's favorites like a boss. #IWannaRockRightNow

These skills of mine don't include cooking, cardio, or camping. Not that camping is really a skill, but seriously, the idea of spending the night in a tent literally terrifies me.

After hanging out with me for over six weeks now, you're fully versed on why cardio isn't my thing; and I'm sure you've identified me as the princess I really am at this point, so the fact that I loathe camping probably doesn't surprise you. But, you may be surprised to note that I'm lacking in cooking skills.

My family is laughing right about now, because "lacking" is really an understatement. I can't cook to save my life. I'm the perfect cast member for *Worst Cooks in America*. Trust me, it's the only way I'm ending up on the Food Network.

The Red Sea does part, and I do get my hands on a recipe every now and then that I can cook up to perfection. My family is rescued by simple recipes.

Some of my go-to's are taco soup, Swiss chicken casserole (y'all, it's sinful, but so good!), and white chicken chili. Email me for the recipes! I will share—I promise.

The only way it is possible to overshadow my lack of cooking skills is to follow every step of a recipe "to the letter" as they say.

I think we can take a lesson from the rescue of the recipe as we're dissecting our good intentions this week. Just like the recipe leads to the rescue, so does bold obedience.

Read Exodus 12, and then come back and let's navigate through these verses together.

The first Passover is a fitting lesson in how obedience leads to the rescue.

God had instructions for Moses and Aaron to give to the Israelites:

> "Take special care of this chosen animal until the evening of the fourteenth day of this first month. Then the whole assembly of the community of Israel must slaughter their lamb or young goat at twilight. They are to take some of the blood and smear it on the sides and top of the doorframes of the houses where they eat the animal."
> – Exodus 12:6-7 (NLT)

And, their obedience led to their rescue:

> So the people of Israel did just as the Lord had commanded through Moses and Aaron. And that night at midnight, the Lord struck down all the firstborn sons in the land of Egypt, from the firstborn son of Pharaoh, who sat on his throne, to the firstborn son of the prisoner in the dungeon. Even the firstborn of their livestock were killed. Pharaoh and all his officials and all the people of Egypt woke up during the night, and loud wailing was heard throughout the land of Egypt. There was not a single house where someone had not died. Pharaoh sent for Moses and Aaron during the night. "Get out!" he ordered. "Leave my people—and take the rest of the Israelites with you! Go and worship the Lord as you have requested."
> – Exodus 12:28-31 (NLT)

Obedience leads to freedom.

We have plenty of clear instructions from God, and when we live those out in bold obedience, He rescues us.

Let's look at a few of God's instructions to us—His simple recipes for living. Draw a line to match the verses with the instructions we're given.

James 1:19-21   Love your enemies.

Matthew 7:7-8   Do not judge others.

Matthew 5:44   Keep on seeking God.

Matthew 7:1   Be slow to speak.

After reading these verses, pick out two that stand out as bold obedience to you where you are today. Jot down particular ways you can obey these instructions (be specific noting the people in your life that will be affected, and situations/circumstances where you can implement this obedience).

_____

_____

_____

_____

_____

If you put the two areas of obedience above into practice, what would that free you from? Write down your thoughts below.

_____

_____

_____

_____

_____

The instructions God has for us are clear in many ways, but the path to obedience is challenging. I love how Paul puts it in Romans. He describes the dilemma we face when it comes to living out bold obedience.

> I have discovered this principle of life—that when I want to do what is right, I inevitably do what is wrong. I love God's law with all my heart. But there is another power within me that is at war with my mind. This power makes me a slave to the sin that is still within me. Oh, what a miserable person I am! Who will free me from this life that is dominated by sin and death? Thank God! The answer is in Jesus Christ our Lord. So you see how it is: In my mind I really want to obey God's law, but because of my sinful nature I am a slave to sin. – Romans 7:21-25 (NLT)

How are you fighting the war in your mind today? How are you letting go of your sinful nature? Below write a prayer committing to steps you are or will take to let go of disobedience in your life.

_____

_____

_____

_____

Overcoming the power within us—the power at war in our minds—is a constant battle we fight. The answer to freedom from fruitless good intentions and our sinful nature is Jesus.

Living out God's recipes of instruction aren't always easy, but there is freedom in obedience.

Enough good intentions. More bold obedience.

We have plenty of clear instructions from God, and when we live those out in bold obedience, He rescues us.

ENOUGH SAID: AFTER READING TODAY'S lesson, let's capture a truth and take a step in obedience.

What did you hear God specifically say to you today through His Word?

_____

_____

_____

_____

How will you respond?

_____

_____

_____

_____

Casseroles Can't Compete

Above all, love each other deeply, because love covers over a multitude of sins.

– 1 Peter 4:8 (NIV)

IN THE SOUTH, WE LOVE our casseroles. Proteins and starches with a little cheese on top cure all.

I grew up in a church where casseroles were pretty much the answer for any life ailment or event.

Death in the family? Let's send a casserole.

New baby? Chicken, cheese, and noodles for mom and dad!

Or my personal favorite, the Church Business Meeting—errrrbody whip up a casserole!

As we're navigating our way through good intentions and bold obedience this week, I think it's the perfect time for a reminder of one of the greatest commandments.

A good casserole gets me only so far on this mission of making disciples.

What really breeds disciples is love.

The people that God has put around us aren't impressed with . . .

O how much Scripture we know

O how many Bible studies we've completed

O how many hours we serve at the church

O how many casseroles we prepare

They look at how we treat others.

Period.

The simplest equation we have for this week's focus is:

217

Bold Obedience = Loving One Another

The barometer is love.

This idea of loving one another was one of Jesus' last instructions to His disciples. Let's look at this in the context of where Jesus and the disciples were when the commandment was handed down.

Judas had just left the room heading to where we now know would be his betrayal of Jesus (John 18:1-11). The Messiah was delivering specific direction to the disciples knowing this was one of the last times He would be with them before His crucifixion.

> "So now I am giving you a new commandment: Love each other. Just as I have loved you, you should love each other. Your love for one another will prove to the world that you are my disciples." – John 13:34-35 (NLT)

Let's focus on two words in this text:

1.   First, let's look at the word "new" in verse 34.

The commandment to love each other was new because the way Jesus loved was a brand new benchmark.

> God showed how much he loved us by sending his one and only Son into the world so that we might have eternal life through him. This is real love—not that we loved God, but that he loved us and sent his Son as a sacrifice to take away our sins. – 1 John 4:9-10 (NLT)

I love how John says . . . *This is real love.* The love of God is foreign to us because it's almost impossible to comprehend. Our human brains can hardly wrap our mind around how wide, how deep, and how unconditional this love is, so it makes sense that our humanity battles to live it out.

Let's take a minute and thank God for His love. Right where you sit say a prayer of thanksgiving for this unimaginable love. Ask God to reveal His love to you in a way that compels you to pour it out to others.

The love of God looks fundamentally different than the way the world represents and manifests love.

Let's compare how the world loves versus how Jesus loves. Jot down characteristics of both types of love in the space below (I've started the list for you, but fill in the space by adding your thoughts):

How the World Loves   **How Jesus Loves**

Performance-based love   The love of Jesus is not earned

_____

_____

_____

How can you take the standard of the way Jesus loves and live that out in bold obedience in your everyday life? List some practical ways below.

_____

_____

_____

_____

2. Now, let's look at the word "prove" in this text.

How we love is the evidence of discipleship in our lives. We cannot claim to be disciples and not love well. And it's important to note that Jesus was speaking to His disciples, pleading with them to love each other, because how we love sets us apart.

> Always be humble and gentle. Be patient with each other, making allowance for each other's faults because of your love. – Ephesians 4:2 (NLT)

Is the way you love setting you apart?

Are you being recognized as a disciple of Jesus by the way you love?

Why or why not?

_____

_____

_____

Sometimes it's easy to fall into the trap of good intentions when it comes to how we love. I see it on social media almost every day. A believer has the best intentions when they're lashing out on a lifestyle or behavior on Facebook, but those social media rants never open up hearts to Jesus.

Good intentions say *they need to know what they're doing is wrong.*

Bold obedience says *love them where they are.*

My sweet sisters, we will never win people over by condemning and criticizing. Loving people where they are is bold, and hard, and downright difficult most days. It's the model we've been given, the commandment to love each other because it's the proof of who we are.

What are some "good intention" traps you fall in when it comes to living out love, and what are some bold steps of obedience you can take to show the world you are a disciple of Jesus by the way you love? Record your thoughts in the spaces below:

"Good Intention" Traps I Fall Into Occasionally   **Bold Steps of Obedience in How I Love**

_____

_____

_____

_____

_____

Love creates harmony among believers and nonbelievers. Tearing people down in judgement never leads to people coming to Jesus, but raising them up in love tells the true story of our soul.

> Above all, clothe yourselves with love, which binds us all together in perfect harmony. – Colossians 3:14 (NLT)

The way we love tells the world who we follow.

We can't escape loving well when it comes to bold obedience. It's the proof in the puddin' of our identity in Christ because love trumps a casserole any day of the week.

Enough good intentions. More bold obedience.

The way we love tells the world who we follow.

ENOUGH SAID: AFTER READING TODAY'S lesson, let's capture a truth and take a step in obedience.

What did you hear God specifically say to you today through His Word?

_____

_____

_____

_____

How will you respond?

_____

_____

_____

_____

Scripture Streaks

I will study your commandments and reflect on your ways. I will delight in
your decrees and not forget your word.

– Psalm 119:15-16 (NLT)

THE BEST PARENTING LEVERAGE MANY of us have over our teenagers is their smart phone. It's an IV they wear that in their minds provides a lifeline to their world. We try to manage and monitor their digital and social media intake, but let's be real, we can't even manage and monitor ourselves well most days.

When these teens of ours find themselves committing a royal screw up, the punishment that typically comes down is the removal of the smart phone from their person. You would think we were taking out a kidney.

Recently our fifteen-year-old took part in some shenanigans with his buddies that left us with no choice but to take his phone for an extended period of time. He's been grounded for four months, and we're still not ready to hand back over the iPhone.

Side note: Can we take a minute and recognize how the grounding of the young ones actually affects us too? I feel like *I've* been grounded for four months. I. Cant. Take. It.

When the gauntlet came down and we pried the phone out of his grimy hands, he hung his head in shame and muttered, "Now all my streaks are gone."

Me: *Huh?*

Said Teenager: *My Snapchat streaks. I'll lose them all.*

Me: *Ummmmm, your what?*

Snapchat streaks? Y'all, who knew this was a thing?

Apparently, teenagers are committed to something other than sleeping 'til noon. They evidently have consecutive days they have "snapped" their friends on Snapchat, and these are called "streaks." Because of our youngest teen's recent mischief, his Snapchat streaks ended without warning. #StreaksNoMore

I am well aware that the word choice for these daily bits of communication leaves a momma begging to know more. After some digging, I am happy to report that these "streaks" are pretty harmless in nature—at least the ones I observed before his friends realized Mom was the one now receiving the daily streaks. They are basically daily snippets of communication, a digital "howdy," if you will, that guarantees the streak continues.

These kids are on a roll with their friend list. And I'm told that if you're one of my streaks that means you hold a special place, but if you break the streak, that's code for "we're done."

My youngest teen was done, and if he ever gets his phone back he will have to start back over with those Snapchat streaks.

Is it possible we can take a lesson from these teenagers and their commitment to not breaking the streak?

When it comes to bold obedience, hanging out in God's Word is critical.

How is our world impacted when we're on a roll in our encounters with Scripture?

What does my life look like when I have a good streak going with getting in the Word every day?

Think about the "streaks" in your life for a minute. What are some things you do, practice, participate in, commit to do every day?

Checking your Facebook feed.

Working out.

Reading your email.

A load of laundry.

Listening to a podcast.

Calling or texting a friend.

Whether we realize it or not, we have streaks of all kinds that we carry out and roll on with every day. Today let's analyze where God's Word falls in our priority of streaks and consider any good intentions we have that can be replaced with bold obedience.

What does your commitment to getting in God's Word look like today? Below jot down how/if you consume Scripture regularly.

_____

_____

_____

_____

We cannot wade through bidding farewell to our good intentions and grabbing hold of bold obedience without acknowledging the fundamental role Scripture plays. Growing in Christ requires the discipline of digging in to God's Word.

> You have been taught the holy Scriptures from childhood, and they have given you the wisdom to receive the salvation that comes by trusting in Christ Jesus. All Scripture is inspired by God and is useful to teach us what is true and to make us realize what is wrong in our lives. It corrects us when we are wrong and teaches us to do what is right. God uses it to prepare and equip his people to do every good work. – 2 Timothy 3:15-17 (NLT)

In these verses, Paul recognizes that the Word corrects us, teaches us, prepares us, and equips us. Below list some ways Scripture has impacted you in these ways in your life. Be specific.

_____

_____

_____

_____

Throughout various seasons of life, my persona in the discipline of reading the Word has fallen into one of the following categories at any given time. Chances are you might recognize yourself in one of these too.

The Newbie – She's either a new believer or a Christian who has yet to discover the impact God's Word can have on her life. Reading the Bible is such a big undertaking, and she doesn't really know where to start.

The Cheerleader – She's proud of her verse of the day and the devotional that shows up in her inbox. She posts them on Instagram and chases every heart button she can get. On a good day it gets read, but there are days when she's running faster to her Facebook feed than to God's Word.

The Taskmaster – She loves checking the box on her Bible Study plan every day. She feels better when the task is completed. Some days the words seep in her soul, and others she walks away forgetting what she's read the minute life comes at her.

The Faithful – She can't wait to hear from God every day. She expects the Holy Spirit to show up and show out when she cracks open her Bible. His Word comes alive in her heart. She prays the Word, meditates on the Word, and Scripture serves as her go-to regarding her choices, her decision-making and the wisdom she prays for daily.

I have been the Newbie.

On Saturdays I'm the Cheerleader.

I'm the Taskmaster on the regular.

But, I'm compelled to be the Faithful. I pray I can be her and stay in her mindset.

What persona best describes your discipline of reading the Word today?

_____

_____

_____

_____

What steps can you take to be more faithful in your discipline of digging in to God's Word? Write down only the steps you are ready to commit to today.

_____

_____

_____

_____

Wherever you fall in your discipline of reading God's Word, chances are you wouldn't even be reading this study right now if you didn't have a heart for more of Him. You showed up here today wanting to hear from Him. Claim that today and commit to one new step of obedience in your faithfulness to His Word.

As we wrap up today, let's dissect the correlation between reading the Word and bold obedience.

> But don't just listen to God's word. You must do what it says. Otherwise, you are only fooling yourselves. For if you listen to the word and don't obey, it is like glancing at your face in a mirror.
> – James 1:22-23 (NLT)

Here's what I know for sure: I can know a lot about God and Scripture, but how I live my life doesn't always correlate to Scripture I've studied.

What has the Word been teaching you recently?

_____

_____

_____

_____

How has that resulted in how you're living your life?

_____

_____

_____

_____

These are tough questions. Important questions. Let's end today with a prayer of asking God to reveal to us how we can connect the Scripture we study to bold obedience in our lives.

Enough good intentions. More bold obedience.

Growing in Christ requires the discipline of digging in to God's Word.

ENOUGH SAID: AFTER READING TODAY'S lesson, let's capture a truth and take a step in obedience.

What did you hear God specifically say to you today through His Word?

_____

_____

_____

_____

How will you respond?

_____

_____

_____

_____

The Prayer Effect

*And we are confident that he hears us whenever we ask for
anything that pleases him.*

– 1 John 5:14 (NLT)

IN MY LATE TWENTIES AND early thirties I was a bridesmaid in nineteen weddings. Nineteen dresses. Nineteen rehearsal dinners. Nineteen wedding days.

I remember throwing oodles of wedding and baby showers for all of my besties. I held back the tears as I ate more cake in that decade than any single girl should.

My friends were celebrating new marriages and new babies, while all I was doing was adding to the wedding bouquet collection at my empty house. I was devastated that God hadn't answered my prayer for a husband and a family.

I thought I was being punished for my first failed marriage and all my rowdy days with my friends in low places. But I kept praying.

I thought God was so busy working in the lives of those around me, showering them with His favor that He had completely forgotten about me. But I kept praying.

I eventually resigned to the fact that a lasting marriage and family wasn't in the cards for me. But I didn't stop praying.

This was my simple prayer: *Lord, bring a man in my life who loves You and will honor You and me.*

Here's an actual excerpt from my prayer journal in late 2001:

Monday, December 17, 2001

Tonight's the first time in over a week I've even sought God through a quiet time or any other time. The holidays are already proving to be tough—as I found myself crying over a TLC Maternity Ward special tonight.

I long for a meaningful relationship—one with God as part of the equation. Lord I know I don't deserve it now—but I have to be honest and say I long for it.

These types of prayers are threaded through my journals over nine years. I kept praying.

When I was thirty-three and had completely given up on finding love again, a charming guy named Coby who I vaguely knew joined my small group at church.

My prayer was finally answered. We dated for a year and married in May of 2008.

That family I had prayed for? Yep, that was part of the package, too. I became a wife to Coby and stepmom to five kids ranging from five to eighteen. Yes, five.

Be careful what you pray for sister! We added one more to the crew in 2010, and our blended family, while nowhere near perfect, represents God's answer to the cry of my heart all of those years.

I didn't realize God had a pretty cool plan for me. It was no mistake that I was raised in a blended family, growing up living with my dad and the best stepmom a girl could ask for. God didn't slip-up when those other relationships I had begged Him to make work out didn't. He had a plan.

I'm so thankful I heard the Holy Spirit whisper through my sin, shame, and brokenness that prayer does matter. Keep praying.

Scripture is full of promises behind the discipline of prayer and stories of how God answers prayer.

Today let's look at Hannah's story.

Read 1 Samuel, chapter 1

Hannah was married to Elkanah, who had two wives, Hannah (who could not have children) and Peninnah (who had children). She was shattered and weary. To make matters worse, Peninnah would irritate and provoke Hannah because she could not get pregnant. #BibleBully

Hannah was so distraught that she would sob and not even eat. But she kept praying.

> Once after a sacrificial meal at Shiloh, Hannah got up and went to pray. Eli the priest was sitting at his customary place beside the entrance of the Tabernacle. Hannah was in deep anguish, crying bitterly as she prayed to the Lord. And she made this vow: "O Lord of Heaven's Armies, if you will look upon my sorrow and answer my prayer and give me a son, then I will give him back to you. He will be yours for his entire lifetime, and as a sign that he has been dedicated to the Lord, his hair will never be cut."

> As she was praying to the Lord, Eli watched her. Seeing her lips moving but hearing no sound, he thought she had been drinking. "Must you come here drunk?" he demanded. "Throw away your wine!"

> "Oh no, sir!" she replied. "I haven't been drinking wine or anything stronger. But I am very discouraged, and I was pouring out my heart to the Lord. Don't think I am a wicked woman! For I have been praying out of great anguish and sorrow."

> "In that case," Eli said, "go in peace! May the God of Israel grant the request you have asked of him."

> "Oh, thank you, sir!" she exclaimed. Then she went back and began to eat again, and she was no longer sad.

> The entire family got up early the next morning and went to worship the Lord once more. Then they returned home to Ramah. When Elkanah slept with Hannah, the Lord remembered her plea, and in due time she gave birth to a son. She named him Samuel, for she said, "I asked the Lord for him." – 1 Samuel 1:9-20 (NLT)

If you read on in First and Second Samuel, you see how Hannah's son Samuel played a vital role in the life of David. Some believe Hannah even influenced Mary, Jesus' mother. Hannah's prayer of praise (1 Samuel 2:1-10) has many similarities to how Mary prayed (Luke 1:46-55). Hannah's commitment to prayer impacted the Kingdom in ways she couldn't have imagined.

We cannot deny that prayer plays a fundamental role in bold obedience. God shows up when we cry out to Him. It might not look exactly like what we had in mind or have the timing we thought was best, but prayer changes everything.

What is your prayer today? Write it below.

_____

_____

_____

_____

We are called to a steady, uninterrupted prayer life. We are called to play our part in the work of God. It is our privilege and responsibility.

What five words describe your prayer life today?

1. _____

2. _____

3. _____

4. _____

5. _____

When our prayers are consistent, the voice of God in our life is constant.

When we have a sense of urgency in our communication with the Father in Jesus' name, we are transformed.

What changes can you make for more consistency and sense of urgency in your prayer life? List practical adjustments you can make in your schedule, your intentions, and/or your commitment to prayer.

_____

_____

_____

_____

_____

Prayer is powerful.

It alters who we are.

Our time with God changes everything.

It is an honor to spend time with the Father. It's our break from our humanity. When we connect with Him we can have assurance that He is listening.

> Because of Christ and our faith in him, we can now come boldly and confidently into God's presence. – Ephesians 3:12 (NLT)

Wishful thinking and positive vibes are great and good, but when we approach the throne of grace boldly and consistently our good intentions shift to brave obedience.

As we've proceeded through this week, we've been reminded that when we exchange our good intentions for bold obedience our purpose comes alive. Let's review how we can propel holiness in how we live through bold obedience.

- O Let's assess our good intentions and remove the barriers between where we are today and where God can use us.
- O Let's find freedom in our brave obedience.
- O Let's recognize that the way we love tells the world who we follow.
- O Let's commit to time in the Word and in prayer so we can transform who we are and become more like Him.

When we have a sense of urgency in our communication with the Father in Jesus' name, we are transformed.

ENOUGH SAID: AFTER READING TODAY'S lesson, let's capture a truth and take a step in obedience.

What did you hear God specifically say to you today through His Word?

_____

_____

_____

_____

How will you respond?

_____

_____

_____

_____

It's time to dig our way out of the pit of good intentions and get brave in our chase after holiness.

Enough good intentions. More bold obedience.

Enough of me. More of Jesus.

Week 8:
Enough *of me*. More JESUS.

Be very careful, then, how you live—not as unwise but as wise, making the most of every opportunity, because the days are evil.

– Ephesians 5:15-16 (NIV)

I SAT AT OUTBACK STEAKHOUSE eating lunch after church one Sunday in the fall of 2014. This tug on my heart to say *enough* had overwhelmed me. Tears ran down my face and onto my coconut shrimp as I poured out my heart to my husband.

It was the culmination of praying and wrestling with God over why I didn't feel like my life was meaning much. I was tired of chasing emptiness and ready for more mission, more purpose. And, this word *enough* was haunting me.

Through my tears I spoke . . .

I feel like I need to do something, write something, or create something around this mandate of enough. I know it sounds weird, but I can't get it out of my head. It creeps back up every single day, and I just don't know what to do, but I can almost feel a physical nudge to take some steps.

I was hoping the hubs would confirm what my flesh had been telling me—*you're really too busy to take on anything else right now. You can't physically or emotionally handle much more. You're already serving in ministry, and it's going great. Adding to that is not really necessary.*

His response was just the opposite.

I think you need to do what you feel God is calling you to do. If that means you write, then write. If that means you do ministry different than you do today, then do it. I've been thinking about this a lot lately, too—you need to do it, Priscilla.

Well, this was news to me. My husband hadn't muttered a word of any of this.

Did it seriously take a bloomin' onion to bring this info to light?

So, I committed to just be faithful with what God was giving me, and take a step. The next day I started on this journey of *enough*. It started as a random blog ministry that I concocted with my marketing skills and the extra five minutes I had before I went to bed each night. I even pulled in my leader in women's ministry to tag along with me. Bless her heart, she walked with me faithfully, but I was really scattered and pretty much all over the place.

In spite of the semi-chaotic state of this journey, it gained a minimal amount of traction, but it soon fell flat. I felt like I was picking up what God was putting in front of me, and even gaining affirmation along the way. But it still felt pretty empty.

Paul's words in Acts 20:24 continued to terrorize me.

> But my life is worth nothing to me unless I use it for finishing the work assigned me by the Lord Jesus—the work of telling others the Good News about the wonderful grace of God. – Acts 20:24 (NLT)

I was compelled to faithful obedience in what God was showing me and encouraging me to do. So, I just kept moving forward with what I had, opportunities He provided, and prayed for a breakthrough.

In early 2017, my dear friend and ministry leader sat across from me at my kitchen table and shared with me what God had put on her heart for the future of the women's ministry she had launched just a few years prior.

I had been praying for some wisdom on what do with my *Enough* project, feeling compelled to move it in a different direction, but not sure what that looked like. When I heard the vision God had put on her heart for the future of the Real Women ministry I was already deeply in love with and a part of, I knew in that moment I was all in.

I shut down the *Enough* blog, but Paul's words still harassed me to the core. God stirred up more craving inside of me to document this tug-of-war between my flesh and my mission.

Was it possible that other women struggled with this too?

Indeed it was.

Was I to write a book? A Bible Study?

I wasn't sure that's where this should go.

I was a writer, but a concept and copywriter—advertising and marketing is my jam, not Bible studies and Christian nonfiction.

Let's be real, my voice doesn't lend itself to perfect grammar. I might even make up words. I love hashtags, and they are not appropriate or grammatically sound in any way, shape, or form in a proper faith-based piece, and the slang that is my Southern dialogue is not an editor's dream. The only Bible curriculum I have ever completed was the required six hours of Old and New Testament at Ouachita Baptist University in 1994.

The obligation in my soul to navigate through this tug-of-war between my flesh and my mission won out over all these reasons I should or could not document this journey of *enough*.

And here we are. You've somehow made it to week eight of this Bible study, and my prayer is that your heart has been ignited to finish the work.

The work of telling others the Good News about the wonderful grace of God. - Acts 20:24b (NLT)

The tug-of-war between our flesh and our mission is won when we say enough of me, more Jesus.

As we wrap up this study this week, let's finish strong. The mantra of our entire journey together has been to say *enough* to all that is standing between where we are today and where God can use us to finish His work.

This week is the grand prize in our quest to say *enough*. The tug-of-war between our flesh and our mission is won when we say *enough of me, more Jesus*. He is the reward, the answer, the replacement to every barrier in the way of our mission.

Enough of my fancy-pants world.

Enough of my selfie centered reality.

Enough of me. More Jesus.

Hello, My Name is Prissy

Just as everyone dies because we all belong to Adam, everyone who belongs to Christ will be given new life.

– 1 Corinthians 15:22 (NLT)

MY GIVEN NAME THAT ADORNS my official state of Arkansas birth certificate is Priscilla Anne Shrader. If you ever met my father, you would know and understand that no one in our family grows up with their official name. We are given nicknames that stay with us through adulthood and beyond.

I grew up Prissy Shrader all my life. Incidentally that is much better than what my brother still endures at the grown-up age of thirty-nine. His official name is Douglas, but we couldn't just have him be Doug. He was unofficially named Willie Clyde by my dad before he was even born, and the name has stuck in all its glory.

Dad told everyone he knew they were naming him Willie Clyde if he was a boy and Willie May if he was a girl, so when he arrived on the scene, family and friends followed suit with what they had been told. It was foreshadowing for all the hazing the youngest in the Shrader clan would endure. #LoveYouMeanItBro

If I'm honest, I guess the name Prissy was appropriate for me on many levels. I have always been an extrovert through and through. I am certainly on the sassy side, and a bit of a princess most days. The name fit, so I wore it with pride.

As I finished junior high and approached high school, I didn't love being Prissy as much. The name might have fit, but I felt like it told my story for me and I didn't necessarily want to be who that name said I was.

239

It might not have been as dramatic as I'm claiming it to be, but needless to say I was done with Prissy by the time I headed to college. The day I arrived on campus, I introduced myself as Priscilla, and never officially referred to myself as Prissy again.

My family all still call me Prissy. It would be weird if they didn't. Old friends from junior high and high school will always know me and refer to me as Prissy. As I get older and my memory fails on a daily basis, this dual identity helps me out in acknowledging how I know folks.

When I get a "Hey Prissy! How are you?" at the grocery store, I know that person is from my high school days. But, when Priscilla is the designation, I know that is an acquaintance I'm certain I came to know as an adult (if you're including eighteen to twenty-two as grown-up status).

Who I was didn't really change when I recaptured my namesake, but my identity certainly shifted. I had grown up. My preceding personality was replaced with who I wanted to be as I walked into the prime of my life.

This Jesus journey we're on is much the same. Christ died that we would receive new life, and in that new life we're called to say goodbye to our old self and come alive in who He is in us.

> Either way, Christ's love controls us. Since we believe that Christ died for all, we also believe that we have all died to our old life. He died for everyone so that those who receive his new life will no longer live for themselves. Instead, they will live for Christ, who died and was raised for them.

> So we have stopped evaluating others from a human point of view. At one time we thought of Christ merely from a human point of view. How differently we know him now! – 2 Corinthians 5:14-16 (NLT)

Think about your new identity in Christ. What are you holding on to from your old self? Consider these categories and jot down traits, qualities, or attributes of yourself that you're holding on to.

Personality Traits:

_____

_____

Sin:

_____

_____

Habits:

_____

_____

Perceptions/Assumptions/Thoughts:

_____

_____

Unraveling our old self and walking in our new identity in Christ is a tug-of-war. Our humanity wants to pursue our own agenda, but we were made for more. The process of dying to our flesh daily is a stroll on the tight rope of life. But sister, we are called to be daughters of His holy priesthood.

Fill in the blanks:

But you are not like that, for you are a _____ people. You are royal priests, a holy nation, God's very own possession. As a result, you can show others the goodness of God, for he _____ you out of the darkness into his wonderful light. – 1 Peter 2:9 (NLT)

What are some ways you feel like God is calling you today? Below list some of the simple callings He's put on your life as you play your role in the holy nation of God's chosen sisters. What are you compelled to do for the Kingdom today?

_____

_____

_____

_____

_____

Now, next to each calling or assignment you listed above, write a simple first step you can take to fulfill that mission, keeping in mind small beginnings are where it's at.

When we take simple steps of obedience in our God assignments, Jesus is becoming alive in us, and our humanity fades. The gospel that is untangling our hearts and compelling us to shout it out to our world is the story of dead souls coming alive. When we say yes to more of Jesus, our numbness fades into blooms of mission.

John the Baptist understood this appeal in his heart to say enough to himself. We reviewed this verse back in week one of this study, but it's too good not to revisit.

> He must become greater and greater, and I must become less and less. – John 3:30 (NLT)

John the Baptist realized the reward was not the glory he received from doing the work of ministry. The real prize was following Jesus.

Day in and day out, I struggle with the reality that so many things are greater than Christ in my life.

The focus of my brain is not always winning souls for Jesus.

My checkbook doesn't always record the wisest use of all that God has given me.

My time is not constantly spent advancing the Kingdom.

My words don't continually honor my Savior.

I fight the battle in my soul, and some days I fall on my face in complete failure.

But y'all, new mercies! Grace for the win! Progress can be slow, but faithfulness is rewarded.

Let's end today with a bold prayer of commitment. Write a prayer below documenting your goal of becoming less and God becoming more.

_____

_____

_____

_____

_____

_____

The purpose isn't perfection. The goal is growth—letting go of ourselves little by little, moment by moment, piece by piece.

Enough of me. More Jesus.

Christ died that we would receive new life, and in that new life we're called to say goodbye to our old self and come alive in who He is in us.

ENOUGH SAID: AFTER READING TODAY'S lesson, let's capture a truth and take a step in obedience.

What did you hear God specifically say to you today through His Word?

_____

_____

_____

_____

How will you respond?

_____

_____

_____

_____

My New Friend Ron

Those who live in the shelter of the Most High will find rest in the shadow of the Almighty.

– Psalm 91:1 (NLT)

MY FIRST JOB OUT OF college was at a trucking company in Little Rock, Arkansas. The nameplate on my cubicle that first day read *Priscilla Shrader – Public Relations Coordinator.* They didn't know much about PR and advertising, and I certainly knew nothing about trucking.

One of my first assignments was to write and produce a training video for their truck drivers about load securement.

Ummmm . . . do you know who you hired?

Keep in mind, in 1994 YouTube was not a thing. I didn't have the luxury of ripping off others' videos like I do today. My first voice over video script would be a detailed explanation on how to safely secure a steel coil onto a flatbed trailer, and I had NO IDEA where to begin.

I was tasked with coordinating the production of the video from start to finish, and they wanted it to be shot at one of their largest customers in Gary, Indiana. Raise your hand if you've ever been to Gary. Let's just say it has never made the top ten destination list on TripAdvisor.

My first adventure in my career in marketing wasn't exactly what I had in mind when I took the job, but they were honest when they said the role would require a variety of responsibilities.

So, I booked a team of videographers and hopped on a plane with the production crew and a driver trainer named Ron who also worked for the company I now called home.

It was my first real experience adulting. #HardHatRequired

Ron was a former truck driver who knew all there was to know about load securement (thank you, Jesus!), and he was challenged with explaining everything to me as we videoed the process of loading forty thousand pound steel coils onto flatbed trailers for two days straight.

I became best friends with the former-trucker-now-driver-trainer who saved my life in more ways than one that week in Gary, Indiana. I'm sure I annoyed the heck out of Ron as I hung on every word and move he made that week.

He was so kind and encouraging, but I'm positive he and the crew had a good laugh or two at my expense. I can't blame them.

I was clueless with a capital C.

When we came back to Little Rock, we began piecing together the video. I pulled it together, completed the video project, and somehow received the sign-off from the Vice President of Safety who had assigned me the task.

The only reason I completed that task was because I had spent valuable time with Ron. The driver trainer who had years of driving experience under his belt knew exactly what I needed to know to complete that video project, and he graciously fed me instruction and wisdom I would never have had on my own.

My time with Ron made the difference in how my assignment was completed.

I'm sure you can see the footsteps of where we're headed today.

Just like my time with Ron impacted my work on that simple video project, our time with Jesus directly impacts our mission. Spending time with Him compels us and equips us to finish the work.

Read Acts 4:1-22.

God had just healed a man who had been a crippled beggar for more than forty years through Peter's proclamation to him to *"get up and walk!"* (Acts 3:6). The religious leaders of that day arrested Peter and John shortly after this incident and brought them before the council of the leaders of religious law. Peter and John pled their case to the council that the man was healed by the *powerful name of Jesus Christ (v. 10)*.

The response of the council is priceless.

> The members of the council were amazed when they saw the boldness of Peter and John, for they could see that they were ordinary

men with no special training in the Scriptures. They also recognized them as men who had been with Jesus. But since they could see the man who had been healed standing right there among them, there was nothing the council could say. – Acts 4:13-14 (NLT)

The council was stunned by the confidence of Peter and John, but that didn't change the fact that they were regular, everyday men with no formal training in religion. What made Peter and John uncommon was the fact that they had been with Jesus.

Sister friend you are capable of meaningful mission because of Jesus. You are not *qualified* to finish His work because of your status, how well you know the Bible, or the fact that you've made fewer mistakes than others. And you are not *unqualified* because of what you've done, who you once were, or where you've been. You are enough forever and always because of a Savior who paid it all.

Just like Peter and John, we can boldly live out our calling to complete the assignments He has given us.

What are you caught up in today that is making you feel unqualified to live out your mission? Jot down your thoughts below.

_____

_____

_____

_____

Don't let the enemy hold your spirit captive any longer with these lies. Pray through your thoughts above one by one and ask God to remove them from your heart and mind, and then draw a line through them, crossing each one out before you move any further.

These verses we're highlighting today in Acts tell us that the council recognized that Peter and John had been with Jesus. Everything about them shined His light, and it could not be ignored.

Have you been with Jesus recently?

Really been with Him?

What does "being with Jesus" look like for you in your life?

_____

_____

_____

_____

My inclination is to drag out my ministry badges of honor when answering questions like this.

I'm in my seat every Sunday morning getting filled up.

I prayed with a friend who is struggling last week.

I tithe every single week.

I haven't missed my small group Bible study all month.

All of these are great—fantastic actually—but they don't mean I've been with Jesus.

The best evidence that Peter and John have been with Jesus is later on in the passage when they responded to the council after the religious leaders commanded them to never again speak or teach in the name of Jesus:

> "We cannot stop telling about everything we have seen and heard."
> – Acts 4:20 (NLT)

Oh how I pray we connect with Jesus so much that we cannot stop telling our world about Him. Let's live with wild abandon, in full out surrender to ourselves, proclaiming who He is. We. Cannot. Stop.

Write a brief prayer of surrender below. Ask God to show you ways you can tell your world about Him.

_____

_____

_____

_____

When we hang out with Jesus we are forever changed, and so are the people around us. The Good News comes alive in our heart and becomes contagious to those we encounter.

Enough of me. More Jesus.

> *When we hang out with Jesus we are forever changed, and so are the people around us.*

ENOUGH SAID: AFTER READING TODAY'S lesson, let's capture a truth and take a step in obedience.

What did you hear God specifically say to you today through His Word?

_____

_____

_____

_____

How will you respond?

_____

_____

_____

_____

Showing Up in the Moments That Count

You must love the Lord your God with all your heart, all your soul, all your strength, and all your mind. And, love your neighbor as yourself.

– Luke 10:27b (NLT)

I'M SURE YOU'RE WELL AWARE (by no choice of your own), that my day job is a huge part of my life. I have quite possibly bored you to tears concerning the ins and outs of my career in advertising, but today I'm asking you to hang with me through one more life lesson I've learned in ad biz.

Consulting with clients on various aspects of their business happens daily in the world of advertising. One of the mantras we preach to our clients is the importance of showing up in the moments that count.

For a business, this means planting your brand along the journey of where your target markets live. Today those destinations include showing up on social and digital media, but any good media mix is full of opportunities to show up in the moments that matter where conversions happen.

Every day God puts moments in our path—opportunities of mission where we can show up and make it count.

Today we're going to look at what might be a familiar story to you and hopefully grab some wisdom.

> The next day there was a wedding celebration in the village of Cana in Galilee. Jesus' mother was there, and Jesus and his disciples were also invited to the celebration. The wine supply ran out during the festivities, so Jesus' mother told him, "They have no more wine."

> "Dear woman, that's not our problem," Jesus replied. "My time has not yet come."

> But his mother told the servants, "Do whatever he tells you."

Standing nearby were six stone water jars, used for Jewish ceremonial washing. Each could hold twenty to thirty gallons. Jesus told the servants, "Fill the jars with water." When the jars had been filled, he said, "Now dip some out, and take it to the master of ceremonies." So the servants followed his instructions.

When the master of ceremonies tasted the water that was now wine, not knowing where it had come from (though, of course, the servants knew), he called the bridegroom over. "A host always serves the best wine first," he said. "Then, when everyone has had a lot to drink, he brings out the less expensive wine. But you have kept the best until now!"

This miraculous sign at Cana in Galilee was the first time Jesus revealed his glory. And his disciples believed in him. – John 2:1-11 (NLT)

First off, can we just chat about this lovely exchange between mother and son? God as a man asking His mom to chill out is fun in so many ways.

Even more entertaining is that she completely ignores His request. We can almost see Jesus roll His eyes when she tells the servants, *"Do whatever he tells you"* (v. 5).

Because the servants listened to Jesus, they had a front row seat to the first recorded miracle He performed. The servants were the first to know. They showed up and did exactly what Jesus said. They knew that wine was not what was poured into those stone water jars.

This man named Jesus with His mom as His plus-one had turned water into wine right before their eyes. I'm certain they were never the same.

What if we hung out in the gospels (Matthew, Mark, Luke & John), read every word day-in and day-out, and did whatever He tells us? I daresay this exercise would fundamentally change who we are.

Read the following verses, and write beside each one what Jesus is telling you to do:

Matthew 4:19 –_____

_____

_____

John 12:36 – _____

_____

_____

Matthew 22:37-39 – _____

_____

_____

Luke 16:9 –_____

_____

_____

When we listen to the instructions of Jesus, we're compelled to show up in the moments that count. His wisdom changes us. We become fully aware that we're called to be different. When we lose ourselves in who He is, all of us is gone and all that remains is His light.

> You see, we don't go around preaching about ourselves. We preach that Jesus Christ is Lord, and we ourselves are your servants for Jesus' sake. For God, who said, "Let there be light in the darkness," has made this light shine in our hearts so we could know the glory of God that is seen in the face of Jesus Christ.
>
> We now have this light shining in our hearts, but we ourselves are like fragile clay jars containing this great treasure. This makes it clear that our great power is from God, not from ourselves. – 2 Corinthians 4:5-7 (NLT)

I'm so grateful I get to see the light of the Lord shine through my sisters in Christ on the regular in women's ministry. Week after week I watch dozens of women who decided to be the light as small group leaders shine brighter than they probably even realize.

It's a beautiful thing to see women of God show up in the moments that count and be the light.

I've witnessed mothers of children with addiction encouraged to keep loving when all they want to do is give up.

I've seen women who have the scar of abortion tattooed on their soul, let go of the shame and remove those wounds through the prayer and support of another sister who has been there done that.

I've hung out in small groups where women have shared how mad they are at God, and leaders have led them back to their identity in Christ in the most meaningful way.

When we call on the power of God in our lives, we lose ourselves and He shines bright.

Have you ever witnessed the light of the Lord shine in someone's heart? Describe that situation or circumstance below.

_____

_____

_____

_____

Do you believe it is possible that God's light can shine through you?

_____

_____

_____

_____

Describe how God's light has or could come alive in your life. Inventory the opportunity of shining God's light in your everyday living below. Where and how can you be the light?

_____

_____

_____

_____

As we conclude today, take a note from the mother of Jesus . . . *Do whatever he tells you.* Because when we seek His face and show up in the moments that count, more of us is gone and His light shines bright.

Enough of me. More Jesus.

When we call on the power of God in our lives, we lose ourselves and He shines bright.

ENOUGH SAID: AFTER READING TODAY'S lesson, let's capture a truth and take a step in obedience.

What did you hear God specifically say to you today through His Word?

_____

_____

_____

_____

How will you respond?

_____

_____

_____

_____

Garage Sale Shenanigans

*And so, dear friends, while you are waiting for these things to happen, make
every effort to be found living peaceful lives that are pure and blameless in
his sight.*

– 2 Peter 3:14 (NLT)

REMEMBER WAY BACK IN WEEK one of this study when I introduced you to
my zany Aunt Jan and her wisdom around hosting a good garage sale?

Quick review:

Aunt Jan was a spitfire with an attitude to match.

She taught me many life lessons, ranging from how to love Jesus to always
order the #1 at the local Mexican restaurant.

She loved God and Oprah—in that order.

And she lived for a good garage sale.

In week one, I failed to introduce you to the crew of characters that tagged
along with her and took part in her garage sale shenanigans. Meet Tommy and
Diane, Aunt Jan's "homies" as she called them. #YouCantMakeThisStuffUp

They were three peas in a pod. For the better part of ten years they were
thick as thieves before Aunt Jan passed away in 2012. They attended church
together, were in the same Bible study group together, and from Thursday night
through Saturday afternoons they would troll the swanky neighborhoods of
Little Rock and its surrounding suburbs in hopes of scoring the deal of the
weekend at all the central Arkansas garage sales.

They each had their own booth at a local flea market where they would
sell most of their garage sale finds, but truth be told they were all candidates

for an episode of *Hoarders* by the junk they collected and didn't sell in their flea market booths.

For years this trio begged me to join in their garage sale rituals on Saturdays, but this girl had no desire to get up at the crack of dawn for someone else's furniture and a kitchen appliance that had never been removed from the box. I was happy sleeping my Saturdays away.

One Friday night I had dinner with Aunt Jan, Tommy, and Diane, and they cornered me.

Before I knew it, I was setting my alarm to head out with them when the sun came up to hit the garage sales. After dinner, they even convinced me to ride with them to "stake out" some of the sales.

We drove slowly by house after house of families preparing for the next day's garage sale. One of the three stooges would jump out and say, "Can we take a quick peek at what you've got to sell?"

We were denied almost every time, but occasionally someone would give us the green light to come check out their sale, and you would have thought it was the pre-Black Friday event of the year. I almost bailed on them after the stake out, but I kept my commitment, and met Aunt Jan at her house at five forty-five that Saturday morning.

I quickly realized they were ready, and I was not. They had wads of one dollar bills and stacks of quarters so they could easily "pay and run" at each garage sale. Diane had a fanny pack the size of Texas, and her hair and makeup were perfection at six a.m. on a Saturday. They each had a list of sales they wanted to hit and a wish list of what they hoped to find.

Off we went on my first adventure to garage sales with this trio.

As we turned on the street of the first house we were going to, I felt the energy in the vehicle change instantly. All three of them unbuckled their seat belts as we turned the corner, and I knew immediately why I had been asked to drive.

The doors of the crew cab truck flew open before I even put it in park. They were off and running. It was a sprint to find the best deal, and I was left in the dust.

In that moment I realized I could probably quit my job and call TLC or A&E with their newest reality show hit.

Y'all, it was like nothing I had seen before. Every stop was funnier and better than the previous. I laughed until I cried, and they never missed a beat.

Needless to say I didn't buy one thing that Saturday, but that garage sale adventure will forever be one of my favorite days.

Aunt Jan, Tommy, and Diane were ready. They were on a mission and they couldn't have been more prepared.

What about you? What are you ready for?

Read Matthew 25:1-13.

This parable of the ten bridesmaids reminds us that we need more of Jesus so we can have the wisdom we need to be ready for His return. The five bridesmaids who had the wisdom to take along extra oil for their lamps were ready when the bridegroom arrived.

Right now, where we are today, what does it look like to be ready in the spiritual sense?

_____

_____

_____

_____

List some aspects of your life that you need to get in order or change to be ready for Christ's return:

_____

_____

_____

In verse twelve of Matthew twenty-five, when the five bridesmaids who had to go out to buy extra oil returned and stood outside the door, the bridegroom proclaims, "Believe me, I don't know you!"

We can live our lives in a way that the bridegroom of Christ will know us well if we remove the parts of us that are overshadowing Jesus in our lives. We can leave behind planted and harvested seeds of mission instead of leaving behind casualties of our emptiness, excuses, distractions, and anxiety.

Review all of the barriers we have covered in this study, and for each category write down anything still standing between where you are today and the mission God has for you. Hopefully we worked through most of them, but I know for me, I have some of the usual suspects that creep up from time to time.

PEOPLE-PLEASING	
EXCUSES	
ANXIETY	
DISTRACTIONS	
LEAVING HIM OUT	
EMPTINESS	
GOOD INTENTIONS	

The enemy would love nothing more than for our flesh to get in the way of God's purpose for our lives. Ask God to remove these barriers, make you aware of when they creep up, and replace them with more of Jesus.

> "Be dressed for service and keep your lamps burning, as though you were waiting for your master to return from the wedding feast. Then you will be ready to open the door and let him in the moment he arrives and knocks. The servants who are ready and waiting for his return will be rewarded. I tell you the truth, he himself will seat them, put on an apron, and serve them as they sit and eat! He may come in

the middle of the night or just before dawn. But whenever he comes, he will reward the servants who are ready. – Luke 12:35-38 (NLT)

Let's be ready with our lamps burning bright.

Enough of me. More Jesus.

We can leave behind planted and harvested seeds of mission instead of leaving behind casualties of our emptiness, excuses, distractions, and anxiety.

ENOUGH SAID: AFTER READING TODAY'S lesson, let's capture a truth and take a step in obedience.

What did you hear God specifically say to you today through His Word?

_____

_____

_____

_____

How will you respond?

_____

_____

_____

_____

It's Time to Finish the Work

Do not despise these small beginnings, for the Lord rejoices to see the work begin.

– Zechariah 4:10a (NLT)

MY SEVEN-YEAR-OLD DAUGHTER HAD HER first sleepover last month. Her best friend lives down the street, and her parents are dear friends, so we agreed this was the perfect scenario for her first sleepover.

She insisted on packing herself. Because her friend's mom knows my momma heart well, I let the packing commence knowing there would be no judgment in what my daughter thought was necessary for her one night away from home.

Before we went out the door, I took inventory of her bag:

1. Pajamas that didn't match – *I did not win the argument that sleepovers were prime time for sporting your best PJs.*
2. Toothbrush and hair brush – *hygiene is important.*
3. Fifty-five stuffed animals – *because you can't bring enough friends to the party.*
4. A throw pillow – *not an actual pillow mind you, but a décor pillow from her room.*
5. A package of goldfish – *a girl's gotta have her snacks.*
6. Her entire nail polish collection – *it's always a good time for a mani-pedi.*
7. The most mismatched outfit she could dig out of her drawers – *it was seriously hideous.*

All of this was stuffed into her rolling Monster High suitcase. #DontJudge

"This is all I've got Mom, will this work?" she shouted before she bolted out the door.

"You better believe it Baby Girl. Let's go!"

And off we went two doors down to her long-awaited first sleepover.

It was a success by the way. That phone call I just knew I would get around eleven p.m. never happened. She grew her wings, and had the time of her life painting her nails, watching movies, and sleeping over with her bestie.

She had lots of stuff in that bag of hers, but none of it made any difference. Fun would have been had either way.

As we wrap up this quest of saying enough to all that is holding us back from getting busy for Jesus, are you finding yourself wondering if what you've got in your bag will work?

Will it be enough?

Can God really use you?

> Jesus saw the huge crowd as he stepped from the boat, and he had compassion on them and healed their sick.
>
> That evening the disciples came to him and said, "This is a remote place, and it's already getting late. Send the crowds away so they can go to the villages and buy food for themselves."
>
> But Jesus said, "That isn't necessary—you feed them."
>
> "But we have only five loaves of bread and two fish!" they answered.
>
> "Bring them here," he said. Then he told the people to sit down on the grass. Jesus took the five loaves and two fish, looked up toward heaven, and blessed them. Then, breaking the loaves into pieces, he gave the bread to the disciples, who distributed it to the people. They all ate as much as they wanted, and afterward, the disciples picked up twelve baskets of leftovers. About 5,000 men were fed that day, in addition to all the women and children! – Matthew 14:14-21 (NLT)

Will what you have in your bag work?

You bet it will, my friend!

Surrender all you've got. He will take it and use it for His glory.

When we say enough of me and pursue more Jesus, it makes no difference what we're bringing to the party. Getting on mission isn't a potluck. It's a feast where He provides everything we need. We're just called to pursue more of Him.

What do you think you need to get on mission that you don't have today? Write your answers in the space below.

_____

_____

_____

_____

I find myself getting in the way of my mission so many times with the belief that I don't have it all together to be on mission.

Then I hear the Holy Spirit whisper, "It's not about you. I am all you need."

So, I drop my anchor where He is and my mission comes calling.

What are you believing today that is holding you back from mission, from fulfilling the purpose God called you to?

_____

_____

_____

_____

I have so loved taking this journey with you. My prayer from the beginning was that your heart would be ignited for His work.

On this quest of saying *enough of me,* I have laughed, cried, and maybe even face-planted a time or two, and I'm really just getting started. I hope more than anything a revival in your heart is burning to finish the work God has called us—to go and make disciples.

Therefore, go and make disciples of all the nations, baptizing them in the name of the Father and the Son and the Holy Spirit. Teach these new disciples to obey all the commands I have given you. And be sure of this: I am with you always, even to the end of the age. – Matthew 28:19-20 (NLT)

Sister, our mission can't wait. I don't know what you're traveling with, what you're bringing to the party, or what you're carrying with you, but it is more than enough and never too much.

Give Him all you've got.

Surrender all that you are, and let's get busy.

It's time to finish the work.

As we've navigated through the tug-of-war between our flesh and our mission this week, we have been constantly reminded that when we say enough to ourselves for more Jesus, everything changes. Let's review how saying enough helps our mission come to life.

- O We are called to say goodbye to our old self and come alive in who He is in us.
- O When we hang out with Jesus we are forever changed, and so are the people around us.
- O We need more of Jesus so we can have the wisdom we need to be ready for His return.
- O When we call on the power of God in our lives, we lose ourselves and He shines bright.

Getting on mission isn't a potluck. It's a feast where He provides everything we need.

ENOUGH SAID: AFTER READING TODAY'S lesson, let's capture a truth and take a step in obedience.

What did you hear God specifically say to you today through His Word?

_____

_____

_____

_____

How will you respond?

_____

_____

_____

_____

The tug-of-war between our flesh and our mission is won through Jesus. Let's get to work.

Enough of me. More Jesus.

EPILOGUE

OUR PRAYER OF *ENOUGH*

What a joy it has been to be on this journey with you. Before you bid farewell to these pages, will you join me in a prayer of surrender to all that is holding us back from our mission?

Father, today I say enough to all that stands between where I am today and where You can use me for Your Kingdom. I pray You would ignite my heart for Your mission. I surrender my excuses, the emptiness I've been chasing for far too long, and the people-pleasing that has held me hostage. I pray You show me how I can invite You into every nook and cranny of my life with bold obedience and clarity in my purpose.

> Teach me your ways, O Lord, that I may live according to your truth! Grant me purity of heart, so that I may honor you. With all my heart I will praise you, O Lord my God. I will give glory to your name forever, for your love for me is very great. You have rescued me from the depths of death. – Psalm 86:11-13 (NLT)

Less of me Lord, and more of You.

Enough of me. More of Jesus.

Amen.

ACKNOWLEDGMENTS

I'm so grateful the Lord put *Enough of Me* on my heart, and even more thankful for every single step He numbered along the way. God placed people in my life who, without even realizing it, left an imprint on this project, and I am forever grateful.

Coby, thank you for being my biggest and best cheerleader not only in this project, but in life. It blows my mind that I get to call you mine. Thank you for reading every word as I wrote and for your encouragement along the way. You challenged me to dig deeper into the Word as I chased after what God has to say about the barriers that stand between where we are today and where God can use us. I know the longs nights and weekends writing took its toll on our family, but you filled all the gaps like a boss. I love you, Big Papa!

Garrett and Noah, thank you for settling for take-out many nights and putting your Netflix binges on hold while I wrote. I'm so grateful I get a front row seat in watching you grow up. Hopefully I didn't embarrass you too much with some of these words, but calling you my bonus sons is one of the joys of my life. I pray I have not and will not let you down. Love you, mean it.

Stella Grace, I am so happy that God picked me to be your mommy. Thank you for checking off the days as I wrote, for praying for me, and for being such a good girl while Mommy worked on this project. I love you to the moon and back, and I just know you're going to change the world with your sassy self. As long as it's for Jesus, it's all good sister.

Mom, thank you for taking me to church and investing in me to be sure I encountered Jesus often. You paid your dues at Sunday School, GA's, and as a church camp counselor. I know I'm not the only fruit from those investments, but this project would not be a reality without the foundation you laid down by putting me in the right places to connect with Jesus.

Dad, thank you for instilling in me that I can do anything (even write a book!) because *everybody puts their britches on the same way I do*. Oh . . . and for teaching me about first downs and pass interference. You are my hero, and I'm so grateful I get to call you Dad.

Stacey, I am so ridiculously thankful for you as a ministry partner, but even more grateful for our friendship. Thank you for covering this project in prayer and for your encouragement from the first publisher meeting to the day I hit send on the final manuscript. You are the best in every way and such an answer to my prayer for a friend who gets me *and* gets Jesus.

Lori and Beverly, thank you for your encouragement, your ideas, your honesty, and feedback through this process. You were two of the firsts I told about this project, and I'm so grateful that you never doubted that God could work—even through my crazy. Thank you for being so gracious with your time.

Christy, Ashley, Marci, Elaine, and all the other prayer warriors (you know who you are!) who lifted this project up. THANK YOU! THANK YOU! There were days when I thought "what the heck am I doing?" And, then I would get a text from one of you asking me how it's going and reminding me that you believed in me and God's vision for this project.

To all the *Real Women* in my life—you were the inspiration for this project. Seeing God work in the lives of women week in and week out is such a gift. I can't wait to dig in to this study with you—it is crazy awesome how God is on the move, and I'm so grateful to be part of His work.

To the team at Ambassador International, thank you for believing in this project and a first-time author with little to no real platform. I'm so grateful for the opportunity, and I greatly appreciate your confidence in my work.

For more information about
Priscilla Peters
&
Enough of Me

please visit:

www.enoughofme.com
www.priscillapeters.com

For more information about
AMBASSADOR INTERNATIONAL
please visit:

www.ambassador-international.com
@AmbassadorIntl
www.facebook.com/AmbassadorIntl

*If you enjoyed this book, please consider leaving us a review on
Amazon, Goodreads, or our website.*

Made in the USA
Columbia, SC
05 January 2025

51095664R00150